Distant Skiddaw viewed from Ashness Bridge

Northern & Central Lake District

CONTENTS

EXPLANATION OF
DEGREE OF DIFFICULTY:
*1: Very Easy, 2: Easy, 3: Easy, 4: Easy to
Moderate, 5: Moderate, 6: Moderate,
7: Moderate to Strenuous, 8: Strenuous,
9: Strenuous, 10: Extremely Strenuous.*

IMPORTANT: Please note that these
gradings and the time lengths quoted
below are based on the personal
experience of the author and may vary
significantly between individual walkers

7/10
4/10
5/10
6.5/10
3/10
6/10
7/10
6/10

WALKED AND WRITTEN BY JOHN WATSON.
SERIES CONCEPT AND DESIGN: MALCOLM PARKER.
ARTWORK AND DESIGN: ANDREW FALLON.

PUBLISHED BY
WALKS OF DISCOVERY LTD.,
1 MARKET PLACE, MIDDLETON-IN-TEESDALE,
CO. DURHAM, DL12 0QG. TEL & FAX: (01833) 640638.

PRINTED IN ENGLAND. ISBN 0-86309-133-4.
COPYRIGHT © WALKS OF DISCOVERY LIMITED 1997.

Northern & Central Lake District

CONTENTS

How to use this Guide

This guide is designed to be used by walkers who have some experience, are appropriately dressed and equipped, and are able to interpret Ordnance Survey Maps.

■ **1** CHOOSE YOUR ROUTE Study the general location map opposite indicating our selection of 18 walk routes, then consult their individual route summary, route description and route map before making your personal choice. Each 'circular' walk starts and finishes at the same point for your convenience.

■ **2** CHECK THE ROUTE SUITABILITY Carefully study your selected route to ensure that it is suitable for you, but particularly the weakest member of your party. To do this also consider the grading system for length and degree of difficulty for each route on the contents pages - as well as the information detailed on each individual walk description.

■ **3** CHECK THE WEATHER CONDITIONS Before you set out it is essential that you check the current and developing weather conditions. In addition, you should consider the Walking and Safety Tips on pages 64 and 65. Also be aware of the telephone numbers of the emergency services.

■ **4** USE WITH AN ORDNANCE SURVEY MAP This guide is designed to be used with the relevant 1:25 000 and 1:50 000 scale O.S. Maps of the area should you so wish. Grid references are used in the guide.

■ **5** USING THE MAP AND ROUTE DESCRIPTION TOGETHER This guide is designed so that the route map and route description can be easily used together with the relevant 1:25 000 Ordnance Survey Map should you so wish. The detailed, concise route descriptions are clearly numbered in both the text and on the route map to help you locate your position.

Beck, tarn and hamlet at delightful Watendlath

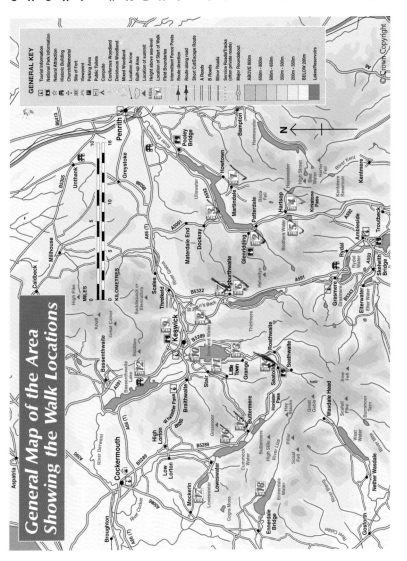

General Map of the Area
Showing the Walk Locations

NORTH & CENTRAL ⑦ LAKE DISTRICT

© Crown Copyright

GENERAL KEY
- ℹ Tourist Information
- 🅿 National Park Information
- ☆ Natural Attraction
- ⚜ Historic Building
- ✚ Church/Memorial
- ⚐ Site of Fort
- 🅿 Parking Area
- 🚻 Public Toilets
- ⚞ Campsite
- Coniferous Woodland
- Deciduous Woodland
- Mixed Woodland
- Built-up Area
- Location Arrow
- Location of summit
- 840m Height above sea-level
- Location of Start of Walk
- Field Boundaries
- Intermittent Fence Posts
- Route direction
- Route along road
- Short Cut/Escape Route
- A Roads
- B Roads
- Minor Roads
- Service Roads/Tracks (often private roads)
- Major Roundabout
- ABOVE 800m
- 650m - 800m
- 500m - 650m
- 350m - 500m
- 200m - 350m
- BELOW 200m
- Lakes/Reservoirs

Summary of all 18 Walks

■ **WALK 1: Hallin Fell** This is often described as the 'forgotten valley' because of its seclusion. Little has changed since Wordsworth praised the beauty of lush meadows and tinkling streams couched within high fells. The outstanding aerial views over Ullswater from the summit of Hallin Fell rewards a steep, but short, climb.

■ **WALK 2: Ullswater** Beginning with a boat trip on the lake from Glenridding, this classic Lakeland walk of scenic splendours returns along Ullswater's eastern shore, via woods, meadows and lower fells. It touches the lakeshore, as well as climbing gently to captivating viewpoints over the lake to distant mountains.

■ **WALK 3: Aira Force** As popular with the Victorians as it is today, this walk can be enjoyed even in the rain. Sheltered by attractive mixed woodland, the route follows the course of Aira Beck and its cascading falls up the valley and out onto grassland round the hamlet of Dockray, returning down the opposite bank of Aira Beck.

■ **WALK 4: Hayeswater** Once through the attractive hamlet of Hartsop, a gradual ascent of Hayeswater Gill with its plunging waterfall leads to remote Hayeswater, a glacial lake tucked away amidst soaring fells. A few wet areas en route around the lake should not impair an opportunity for quiet contemplation of scenic grandeur.

■ **WALK 5: Brothers Water** Lakeland's smallest lake, a gem set in the Hartsop valley, lies at the centre of this gentle walk through embracing woods and meadows with open vistas of encircling towering mountain peaks. A slight diversion to view the historic cottages and farmsteads of the attractive hamlet of Hartsop is recommended.

■ **WALK 6: Thirlmere** The outward route on a terraced path along the lower slopes of the Helvellyn range is liberally sprinkled with streams and waterfalls and provides an elevated viewpoint over Thirlmere. The return along the 'drowned' valley hugs the eastern lakeshore, amply endowed with a rich variety of mixed woodland.

■ **WALK 7: Naddle Fell** On a fine day after a short, sharp climb, this modest undulating fell is a place to wander, browse, drink in its charm and view distant mountains. The tiny church of St John's in the Vale is worth a visit before returning via a delightful, elevated path above St John's Beck.

■ **WALK 8: Castlerigg Stone Circle** The bowl of the Naddle valley provides a marvellous vantage-point for open views of mountain heights. Traversing low fell and lush pastureland, the walk encounters minuscule, isolated Tewet Tarn, a well-preserved ancient stone circle, and a small church with an interesting history.

■ **WALK 9: Latrigg** A pleasant amble through the mixed woodland of Greta Gorge affords near and elevated views of the River Greta. A gradual climb through farmland emerges on the airy, grassy heights of Latrigg with spectacular views over Keswick and Derwent Water, not lost in a gentle zig-zag descent into Keswick.

■ **WALK 10: Ashness Bridge** A walk which takes in renowned Lakeland viewpoints. From Keswick, a lovely path skirts the tree-fringed eastern shore of Derwent Water. Photogenic Ashness Bridge, a short climb, and an escarpment stroll to Walla Crag with impressive views over Derwent Water, leaves an easy descent via woods and fields.

■ **WALK 11: Cat Bells** An enchanting walk with unsurpassable views across Derwent Water from on high and from its western shore. The short, steep climb onto Cat Bells ridge is rewarded by sublime all-round vistas. A steady descent to the lakeside, and a parkland amble round its bays, brings a leisurely end to a memorable walk.

■ **WALK 12: Mirehouse** A terraced forest path with fine aerial views over Bassenthwaite Lake drops down through verdant pastures to tiny St Bega's Church in its lovely lakeshore setting. Options available are a visit to the C17th manor house and its gardens, and/or a lakeside stroll which inspired Tennyson's 'Morte d'Arthur'.

■ **WALK 13: Watendlath** A beguiling beckside browse through mixed woodland and beside open fell encounters two literary inspirations in dramatic Lodore Falls and the picturesque hamlet of Watendlath and its tarn. A gradual climb onto airy ridges with panoramic views, followed by a wooded valley descent, ends an unforgettable walk.

■ **WALK 14: Castle Crag** A walk, with a brief ascent and descent which require

care, reveals the natural beauty surrounding the jaws of Borrowdale. Encountered en route are sheer jagged crags, broadleaved woodland, verdant pastures, the tumbling River Derwent, plus magnificent aerial views from the rocky plinth of Castle Crag.

■ **WALK 15: Buttermere** This lakeside amble, fashionable with the Victorians, is regarded as one of the finest circuits in the Lake District. The towering rugged mountains which embrace the lake are mirrored in its green glassy waters, and throughout provide awe-inspiring upward views from its tree-fringed shore.

■ **WALK 16: Rannerdale** The steady climb up this hidden valley of bluebell-clad lower slopes and sparkling rivulets is followed by a gradual fellside descent with superb views over the vale of Buttermere and its surrounding mountains. The return from Buttermere village is via fields, wood, and lower fell above scenic Crummock Water.

■ **WALK 17: Loweswater** Tranquillity is the hallmark of this stroll round an oft-forgotten lovely lake bordered by a rich variety of hardwoods and flower-bedecked pastures. Here is an opportunity to browse at leisure through a soft landscape of Skiddaw Slate with open views of the encircling, grassy low fells.

■ **WALK 18: Ennerdale Water** Time is required for the circuit of a crystal-clear lake set in a peaceful valley. An easy meander along its conifer-clad southern shore belies the slower progress on a rocky path along its northern fringes and a short scramble over Anglers Crag. Spell-binding views and serenity reward any effort expended.

WALK 1

LANTY TARN - ST MARTIN'S CHURCH - HAUSE FARM - HALLIN FELL

2.8 MILES (4.5 km)

Route Details

Distance	2.8 miles (4.5 km)
Degree of Difficulty	Easy
Ascent	217m (712ft)
Time	2.5 hours

Start and Finish Points

Small lay-by car park opposite St Peter's Church (GR 435192) at the head of Martindale.

From Pooley Bridge take the minor road south-west for 4.4 miles (7 km). It follows the eastern shore of Ullswater, by-passing the hamlet of Howtown. After a series of uphill hairpin bends the car park is on the right at the top of the rise.

Maps Needed

OS Outdoor Leisure No 5 (1:25 000)
OS Landranger No 90 (1:50 000)

Parking Facilities

As well as the car park opposite St Peter's Church (GR 435192) there is also a grass verge parking area (GR 434186) opposite St Martin's Church, so the walk could start and finish at (5).

Route Description

■ **1** Start by crossing the road from the parking area. Follow the bridleway sign on the right along a broad path with St Peter's Church on the left. The path bends right along a wall on the right to a sharp left bend.

■ **2** Fork right, off the main path, at the bend. Pass minuscule Lanty Tarn on the left.

■ **3** Go straight ahead where the wall bends right. Follow a narrow stony path, contouring below a rocky outcrop up on the left. Continue with a wall on the right to the wall corner.

■ **4** Bear diagonally right, down from the wall corner. Follow a zig-zagging broad grassy path down the fellside. Aim to emerge on the minor road at a point just right of St Martin's Church below.

■ **5** Turn left, along the road, past St Martin's Church, bending right across Christy Bridge over Howegrain Beck. Proceed to just past Winter Crag Farm on the right where the road bends left.

■ **6** Turn right, off the road, at a bridleway sign with the farm on the right. Follow a broad undulating track, Sessions Road, which bends left to the Sandwick Road.

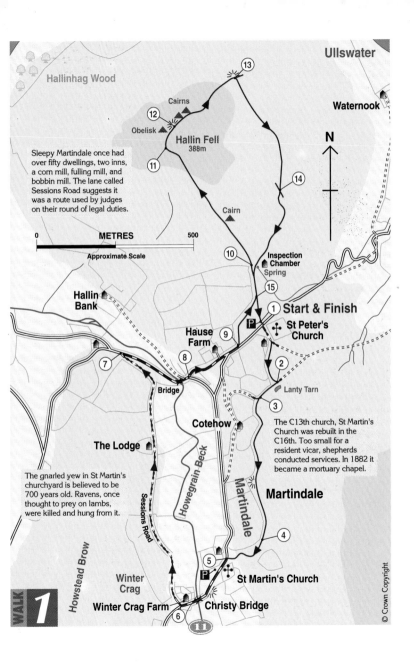

Ullswater

Hallinhag Wood

Cairns

Obelisk ▲

Hallin Fell
388m

Waternook

N

Sleepy Martindale once had over fifty dwellings, two inns, a corn mill, fulling mill, and bobbin mill. The lane called Sessions Road suggests it was a route used by judges on their round of legal duties.

Cairn ▲

0   METRES   500

Approximate Scale

Inspection Chamber
Spring

Hallin Bank

Start & Finish

P

St Peter's Church

Hause Farm

Bridge

Cotehow

Lanty Tarn

The C13th church, St Martin's Church was rebuilt in the C16th. Too small for a resident vicar, shepherds conducted services. In 1882 it became a mortuary chapel.

The Lodge

Martindale

The gnarled yew in St Martin's churchyard is believed to be 700 years old. Ravens, once thought to prey on lambs, were killed and hung from it.

Howstead Brow

Winter Crag

Winter Crag Farm

St Martin's Church

P

Christy Bridge

11

WALK 1

Christy Bridge over Howegrain Beck in Martindale

■ **7** Turn sharply right down the road, bending left across a bridge over Howegrain Beck, then right.

■ **8** Bear left at a fork. Follow the road uphill, passing Hause Farm on the left.

■ **9** Turn left, off the road, at the wall corner on the left after the farm. Follow the wall, bending right up the fellside to the wall corner.

■ **10** Go ahead, leaving the wall and bending slightly left. Continue uphill on a broad grassy path, passing a large cairn on the right. Ignore any paths coming in from either side.

■ **11** Turn right on reaching a small grassy plateau at the crest of the ascending path. Make a short climb up to the summit of Hallin Fell (388m/1273ft), marked by a large square stone obelisk.

■ **12** Descend right from the summit. Proceed for 50m. Bear left down a narrow ravine from the two small cairns on the left at its head. Descend for 200m towards Ullswater below.

■ **13** Turn right at the foot of the ravine, ignoring the downhill path ahead. Follow a level path for 300m, bending right onto a grassy saddle. Descend ahead.

■ **14** Follow the wider path at cross-paths, descending steeply. The path winds left, then curves right. Pass a low concrete inspection chamber on the left. Proceed for another 20m to the wall below near (10). Turn left on the outward path with the wall on the right to where it bends right.

■ **15** Go straight ahead down the grassy fellside to emerge on the minor road with the car park on the left.

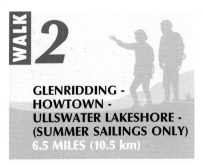

WALK 2

GLENRIDDING - HOWTOWN - ULLSWATER LAKESHORE - (SUMMER SAILINGS ONLY)

6.5 MILES (10.5 km)

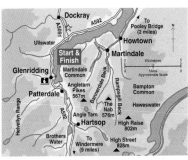

Route Details

Distance	6.5 miles (10.5 km)
Degree of Difficulty	Moderate
Ascent	185m (607ft)
Time	5 hours

Start and Finish Points

Car park at the Ullswater steamer pier (GR 389169) off the A592 at Glenridding village. (Sailings are summer only. For up-to-date sailing times telephone Ullswater Navigation Company 017684 82229). Glenridding is on the A592 Penrith to Windermere road, 13 miles (21 km) south-west of Penrith along the western shore of Ullswater, and 13 miles (21 km) north of Windermere over Honister Pass.

Maps Needed

OS Outdoor Leisure No 5 (1:25 000)
OS Landranger No 90 (1:50 000)

Parking Facilities

Car park (GR 389169). There is also a large car park (GR 386170) in the centre of Glenridding village adjacent to the Tourist Information Centre.

Route Description

■ **1** Start by taking the boat from the steamer pier at Glenridding. Disembark at Howtown pier (GR 443199).

■ **2** Turn right on a lakeshore path. Cross a footbridge. Go through a kissing-gate. Pass through another kissing-gate to follow a lakeshore tarmac track for 100m.

■ **3** Turn left through a kissing-gate at a signpost to Patterdale/Sandwick. Ascend steps along a wall on the right.

■ **4** Turn right at the top at a footpath sign. Go behind Waternook Cottage. Follow an ascending path along the lower slopes of Hallin Fell with a wall on the right and the lakeshore below. Bend left over Geordie's Crag.

■ **5** Pass through a kissing-gate to enter Hallinhag Wood. The undulating path keeps just above the shoreline down on the right.

■ **6** Go through a kissing-gate to join the lakeshore at Sandwick Bay. Pass through a wall gap 20m ahead. Go through a wicket-gate adjacent to a field-gate to emerge from the wood. Follow across three narrow fields away from the lakeshore, passing through three wicket-gates. Curve right to cross a footbridge over Sandwick Beck. Go

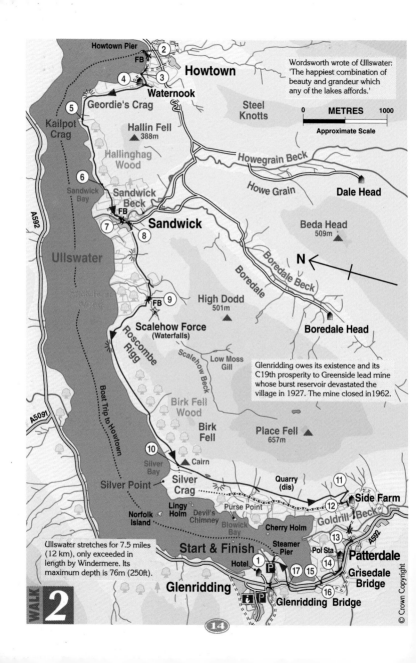

Howtown Pier

② FB

③

Howtown

④

Waternook

⑤ Geordie's Crag

Kailpot Crag

Hallin Fell ▲ 388m

Steel Knotts

Wordsworth wrote of Ullswater: 'The happiest combination of beauty and grandeur which any of the lakes affords.'

0   METRES   1000
Approximate Scale

Hallinhag Wood

Howegrain Beck

Howe Grain

Dale Head

⑥

Sandwick Bay

Sandwick Beck

FB
⑦ ⑧

Sandwick

Beda Head 509m ▲

A592

Ullswater

Boredale Beck

Boredale

FB ⑨

Scalehow Force (Waterfalls)

High Dodd 501m ▲

N ←

Boredale Head

Roscombe Rigg

Scalehow Beck

Low Moss Gill

Glenridding owes its existence and its C19th prosperity to Greenside lead mine whose burst reservoir devastated the village in 1927. The mine closed in 1962.

Boat Trip to Howtown

A5091

Birk Fell Wood

Birk Fell

Place Fell ▲ 657m

⑩ ▲ Cairn

Silver Bay

Quarry (dis)

⑪

Silver Crag

Silver Point

Lingy Holm   Devil's Chimney

Purse Point

⑫ Side Farm

Goldrill Beck

Norfolk Island

Blowick Bay

Cherry Holm

⑬

Start & Finish

Steamer Pier

Pol Sta

⑭ Patterdale

Ullswater stretches for 7.5 miles (12 km), only exceeded in length by Windermere. Its maximum depth is 76m (250ft).

Hotel P

① ⑰ ⑮

Grisedale Bridge

Glenridding

P

Glenridding Bridge

⑯

Glenridding Bridge

© Crown Copyright

WALK 2

14

through a field-gate into the hamlet of Sandwick.

■ **7** Turn left up the minor road and continue along it for 100m.

Ullswater from Glenridding shoreline

■ **8** Turn right, off the road, at the last of the cottages on the right at a sign to Patterdale. Ascend the path along a wall on the right with the lakeshore far below fields on the right. Continue ahead, downhill, bearing right at a fork with the wall on the right.

■ **9** Cross a footbridge over Scalehow Beck with Scalehow Force (waterfalls) up on the left. The uphill path continues with the wall on the right. It turns right with the wall, descending and bending left round Roscombe Rigg. Pass through Birk Fell Wood, skirting the shoreline down on the right. Proceed as far as a junction marked by a very large cairn with Silver Point over to the right.

■ **10** Fork left, off the shoreline path. Go up a stony path and through a narrow path. Ahead, the high path gradually descends. Ignore a right fork. Bear left on a shelf path, crossing a bed of loose slates in a disused quarry.

■ **11** Double back sharp right down the fellside along a wall on the left.

■ **12** Turn left onto a broad path at the bottom. Pass through a field-gate in the yard of Side Farm. Turn right between the farmhouse on the left and a barn on the right. Go through a field-gate to exit from the farmyard. Continue on a track. Pass through two kissing-gates adjacent to cattle-grids. Cross a footbridge over Goldrill Beck. Ahead, the track emerges onto the A592 in Patterdale village.

■ **13** Turn right on the pathway along the road on the left, passing the Police Station on the right. Continue ahead to cross Grisedale Bridge. Proceed for 100m.

■ **14** Filter right onto a loop path through a thin belt of trees parallel to the road on the left. Rejoin the A592 after 200m. Cross the road.

The hamlet of Howtown on Ullswater

■ **15** Turn right. Proceed for 100m.

■ **16** Filter left at a permissive footpath sign. Follow an undulating loop path through woodland, skirting the road down on the right. Turn right down steps to rejoin the A592.

■ **17** Cross the road. Pass through a wicket-gate opposite. The path ahead bends left over grassland with the lakeshore on the right. Enter the car park.

WALK 3

AIRA FORCE - HIGH FORCE - RIDDINGS BECK - DOCKRAY -

3.5 MILES (5.6 km)

Route Details

Distance	3.5 miles (5.6 km)
Degree of Difficulty	Easy
Ascent	129m (423ft)
Time	2.5 hours

Start and Finish Points

Aira Force National Trust car park (GR 401201) off the A592 at the corner of the junction with the A5091.
Aira Force is off the A592 Penrith to Windermere road, 10.5 miles (17 km) south-west of Penrith along the western shore of Ullswater, and 16.5 miles (26.5 km) north of Windermere over Honister Pass.

Maps Needed

OS Outdoor Leisure No 5 (1:25 000)
OS Landranger No 90 (1:50 000)

Parking Facilities

Aira Force National Trust car park (GR 401201). There is also a small car park (GR 398206) off the A5091. It is possible to follow a waymarked path down from the rear of the car park, joining the route above (4) at the seat.

Route Description

■ **1** Start from the top left corner of the car park. Pass through a wicket-gate adjacent to a field-gate onto a gravelled pathway between fences. Proceed for 150m.

■ **2** Turn right through a wicket-gate. Go ahead to cross a footbridge. Pass through a fence gap. Descend steps. Cross another footbridge. Ascend steps up the bank opposite, bending left.

■ **3** Fork left, following a wooded terraced path with Aira Beck below to the left. The path descends to cross a slate bridge below Aira Force (waterfall).

■ **4** Turn left up steps, curving right to a junction at a bench-seat. Turn right, on a broad path, bending right to a slate bridge spanning the lip of Aira Force.

■ **5** Turn left before the path crosses the bridge. Follow upstream through trees with Aira Beck on the right. Pass through a wicket-gate. At a fork, bear left up a broad path leading slightly away from the beck. Descend to Aira Beck. Cross a gated footbridge.

■ **6** Go half-right up a bankside path. Filter left at the top. Continue upstream with Aira Beck on the left to High Force (waterfall). Ascend away from the beck. Pass through a wall-gate signed to

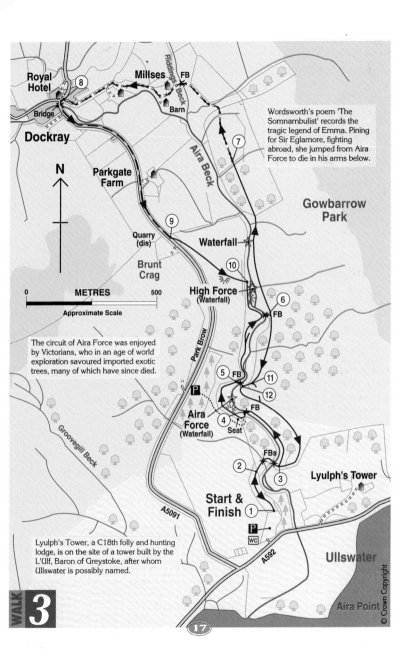

Royal Hotel

⑧

Millses

FB

Riddings Beck

Barn

Bridge

Dockray

Aira Beck

⑦

Wordsworth's poem 'The Somnambulist' records the tragic legend of Emma. Pining for Sir Eglamore, fighting abroad, she jumped from Aira Force to die in his arms below.

N

Parkgate Farm

⑨

Quarry (dis)

Waterfall

Gowbarrow Park

Brunt Crag

⑩

High Force (Waterfall)

⑥

FB

0   METRES   500

Approximate Scale

Park Brow

The circuit of Aira Force was enjoyed by Victorians, who in an age of world exploration savoured imported exotic trees, many of which have since died.

⑤ FB

⑪

P

⑫

FB

Aira Force (Waterfall)

④

Seat

Groovegill Beck

FBs

②

③

Lyulph's Tower

Start & Finish ①

P

WC

A5091

A592

Ullswater

Lyulph's Tower, a C18th folly and hunting lodge, is on the site of a tower built by the L'Ulf, Baron of Greystoke, after whom Ullswater is possibly named.

Aira Point

© Crown Copyright

WALK **3**

17

Aira Beck on a tumbling journey over High Force

Dockray and Ulcat Row. Continue on a gradual ascent to cross over a rivulet through a broken wall. Emerge from trees onto a broad green path over open fell.

■ **7** Continue ahead and go through a gate at a signpost. Bear left, down the path, to a corner of a fenced field. Turn right, along the fence on the right. The path widens, bending left. Cross a planked bridge. Continue uphill between a cottage and a barn. Pass through a field-gate. The track leads into the hamlet of Dockray, joining the A5091 opposite the Royal Hotel.

■ **8** Turn left on the road signposted to Ullswater and Patterdale. Cross the road bridge over Aira Beck. Continue on the road, downhill for 650m, keeping a careful eye out for traffic.

■ **9** Filter left, off the road, into a lay-by, opposite a restricted quarry parking area on the right. Exit from the lay-by through a kissing-gate. Descend a permitted grassland path. Go through another kissing-gate in a wire fence near the bottom of the slope. Pass through a wall gap opposite to emerge at High Force.

■ **10** Turn right along Aira Beck on the left. Turn left over the gated footbridge previously crossed to (6). Turn sharp right along a wall on the right. Climb up a stony stepped path, curving right high above a ravine with Aira Beck below to the right.

■ **11** Fork half-right, off the path, near the bottom of the slope. Go through a wicket-gate in a wire fence. Arrive at the bridge over the lip of Aira Force.

■ **12** Do not cross the bridge. Turn left, ignoring a fork down right. Stay on the high level path, bearing round right to emerge from trees. The path descends through a wicket-gate to join a path at (3). Follow the outward route to return to the car park.

WALK 4

HARTSOP - HAYESWATER GILL FALLS - HAYESWATER - WATH BRIDGE
4.8 MILES (7.8 km)

Route Details

Distance	4.8 miles (7.8 km)
Degree of Difficulty	Moderate
Ascent	250m (820ft)
Time	3.5 hours

Start and Finish Points

Cow Bridge car park (GR 410134) off the A592.
Cow Bridge car park is situated 700m north-west of Hartsop village, off the A592 Penrith to Windermere road. It is 15.5 miles (25 km) south-west of Penrith, along the western shore of Ullswater and through the villages of Glenridding and Patterdale, and 10.5 miles (17 km) north of Windermere over Honister Pass.

Maps Needed

OS Outdoor Leisure No 5 (1:25 000)
OS Landranger No 90 (1:50 000)

Parking Facilities

Cow Bridge car park. Because of the narrow access road to Hartsop, visitors are not encouraged to take cars into this confined village.

Route Description

■ **1** Exit from the top left corner of the car park onto the A592. Cross the road. Turn right. Proceed along the road for 250m.

■ **2** Turn left, off the A592, at a telephone kiosk onto a narrow minor road, signposted to Hartsop. Follow the road, bending right through Hartsop. Fork right at the end of the village. Go straight across a restricted riverside parking area.

■ **3** Pass out of the parking area through a kissing-gate adjacent to a field-gate. Go straight ahead at a pathway junction, following the bridleway sign to Hayeswater. Pass a cluster of wooden sheepfolds on the right. The broad track becomes a tarmac fell track up the hillside. Pass through a field-gate after 600m.

■ **4** Ahead, fork left up the tarmac fell track along a high wall on the left and Hayeswater Gill below on the right. Go through a field-gate after 225m. Continue uphill to a water filter house.

■ **5** Fork right down to a wall below the water filter house. Cross a diagonally-stepped stone stile. Immediately cross a footbridge.

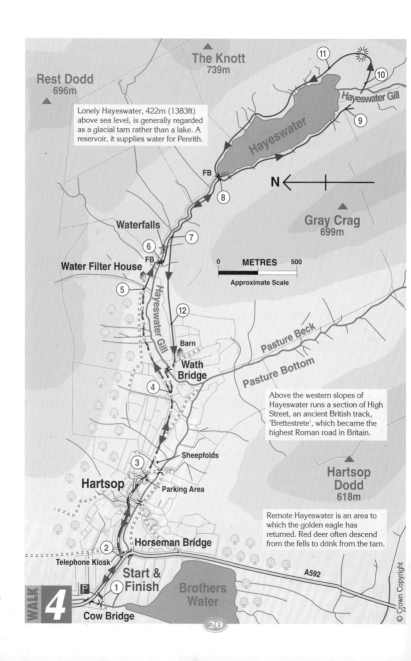

The Knott
739m

Rest Dodd
696m

Lonely Hayeswater, 422m (1383ft) above sea level, is generally regarded as a glacial tarn rather than a lake. A reservoir, it supplies water for Penrith.

Hayeswater

Hayeswater Gill

⑪
⑩
⑨

FB
⑧

N ←

Waterfalls
⑦
⑥ FB
Water Filter House
⑤

Hayeswater Gill

Gray Crag
699m

0   METRES   500
Approximate Scale

⑫

Barn

Pasture Beck

Pasture Bottom

Wath
Bridge

④

Above the western slopes of Hayeswater runs a section of High Street, an ancient British track, 'Brettestrete', which became the highest Roman road in Britain.

Sheepfolds

③

Hartsop

Parking Area

Hartsop
Dodd
618m

Remote Hayeswater is an area to which the golden eagle has returned. Red deer often descend from the fells to drink from the tarn.

Horseman Bridge

②

Telephone Kiosk

Start &
① Finish

Brothers
Water

A592

WALK

4

P

Cow Bridge

© Crown Copyright

■ **6** Turn left up a stony path with the waterfalls of Hayeswater Gill on the left. Proceed uphill for 300m.

■ **7** Filter left onto a broad uphill path. Proceed for 500m to the top of the rise.

■ **8** Do not cross the footbridge at the foot of Hayeswater Gill on the left. Go ahead on a narrow grassy path, bordering the western shore of Hayeswater. After 900m, at the head of the lake, the path peters out.

■ **9** Bear diagonally left towards a large whale-backed grassy mound in the foreground of a cluster of grassy humps which form a glacial drumlin field. Cross a broken wall after 150m. Go ahead to ford the Hayeswater Gill and arrive at the large grassy mound.

■ **10** Pass round behind the mound, bending left. With no path over rough grassland, aim for the south-east corner of Hayeswater, keeping in a high arc and bending left to avoid marshy ground.

■ **11** Pick up a distinct narrow path. Follow it along the eastern shore of Hayeswater. Bend left at the foot of the lake across the footbridge to arrive at (8). Turn right on the broad downhill path. Fork left at (7). Proceed ahead for another 600m.

■ **12** Pass through a kissing-gate adjacent to a field-gate. Go ahead through a field-gate with a barn on the left. The track curves down right across Wath Bridge over Hayeswater Gill. Ahead, uphill, the track arrives at (4). Retrace the outward route to the car park.

The picturesque and historic hamlet of Hartsop

WALK 5

GOLDRILL BECK - BROTHERS WATER - BROTHERSWATER INN - HARTSOP

2.7 MILES (4.3 km)

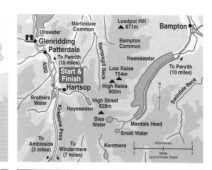

Route Details

Distance	2.7 miles (4.3 km)
Degree of Difficulty	Very Easy
Ascent	45m (147ft)
Time	2 hours

Start and Finish Points

Cow Bridge car park (GR 403134).
It is situated off the A592 Penrith to
Windermere road, 15.5 miles (25 km)
south-west of Penrith, along the western
shore of Ullswater through the villages of
Glenridding and Patterdale. It is on the
right 1.7 miles (2.8 km) beyond
Patterdale.
From Windermere it is 10.5 miles (17
km) north over Honister Pass, and is on
the left 300m after the right junction
signposted to the village of Hartsop.

Maps Needed

OS Outdoor Leisure No 5 (1:25 000)
OS Landranger No 90 (1:50 000)

Parking Facilities

The car park at Cow Bridge (GR
403134) is the only car park available
for this walk.

Route Description

■ **1** Start to the right of walled Cow
Bridge over Goldrill Beck at the top
right-hand southern corner of the car
park. Go through a kissing-gate
adjacent to a field-gate. Proceed ahead
along a lane, through woodland with
reeded Goldrill Beck to the left.
Continue with the west bank of
Brothers Water below on the left.
■ **2** Pass through a kissing-gate
adjacent to a field-gate opposite the
head of the lake. Go through a kissing-
gate adjacent to a field-gate and follow
the lane ahead towards Hartsop Hall
Farm.
■ **3** The lane goes right of the farm,
bending left round farm buildings. Pass
between a wall and a tree behind the
farmhouse. Turn right through a gate
adjacent to a cattle-grid.
■ **4** Follow the straight farm driveway
through pastureland. Cross a
footbridge over Kirkstone Beck.
Ahead, pass through a gate adjacent
to a cattle-grid. Continue ahead
through the centre of a campsite. Pass
through a gate with a campsite shop
on the left. Go ahead up a tarmac
driveway for 75m with access to
Brotherswater Inn up on the right.

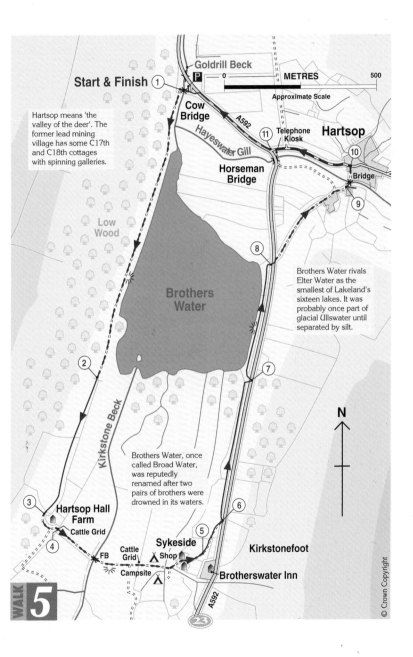

Goldrill Beck

Start & Finish ①

METRES · 0 · 500
Approximate Scale

Cow Bridge

A592

Haysewater Gill

⑪ Telephone Kiosk

Hartsop

⑩

Hartsop means 'the valley of the deer'. The former lead mining village has some C17th and C18th cottages with spinning galleries.

Horseman Bridge

Bridge

⑨

Low Wood

Brothers Water

⑧

Brothers Water rivals Elter Water as the smallest of Lakeland's sixteen lakes. It was probably once part of glacial Ullswater until separated by silt.

②

Kirkstone Beck

⑦

N

Brothers Water, once called Broad Water, was reputedly renamed after two pairs of brothers were drowned in its waters.

③ **Hartsop Hall Farm**

Cattle Grid

④

FB

Cattle Grid

Campsite

⑤ Sykeside
Shop

Kirkstonefoot

⑥

Brotherswater Inn

A592

23

WALK 5

© Crown Copyright

Reeds grace the shores of tiny Brothers Water

■ **5** Fork left, continuing up the driveway to its junction with the A592. Do not cross the road.

■ **6** Turn left through a wicket-gate. Follow a narrow well-made permissive footpath signed to Brothers Water. This passes a wall on the right and a wire field boundary fence on the left, below the A592. Proceed for 450m. Pass through a wall gap at the end of the footpath to rejoin the A592. Do not cross the road.

■ **7** Turn sharp left, down a narrow wooded path, away from the road, at a ground-level sign to the Lake and Hartsop. The path meanders along the shoreline through trees. Pass through a kissing-gate in a fence. Bear right up the path over meadowland, away from the lake, towards the road. Pass through a kissing-gate to emerge immediately onto the A592.

■ **8** Bear diagonally right across the busy road with caution to a wall sign to Hartsop. Turn left up a broad walled path bending right to join Hayswater Gill on the left.

■ **9** Fork left down to the gill. Cross a narrow metal bridge over the gill. Pass between barns ahead onto a minor road. (Turn right up the road to visit the pretty and historic hamlet of Hartsop).

■ **10** Turn left down the road. Proceed as far as the junction with the A592 where there is a telephone kiosk on the left.

■ **11** Turn right along the tarmac footpath on the right side of the road. Proceed for 300m. Turn left across the busy road with caution and enter the car park.

WALK 6

STY BECK FALLS - FISHER PLACE GILL FALLS - THIRLMERE LAKESHORE - GREATHOW WOOD

4.7 MILES (7.6 km)

Route Details

Distance	4.7 miles (7.6 km)
Degree of Difficulty	Easy
Ascent	120m (394ft)
Time	3 hours

Start and Finish Points

Legburthwaite picnic area and car park (GR 318195), off the B5322.
It is situated off the B5322, 3.5 miles (5.6 km) south from the junction with the A66 at Threlkeld and 650m from the junction with the A591.

Maps Needed

OS Outdoor Leisure No 4 (1:25 000)
OS Outdoor Leisure No 5 (1:25 000)
OS Landranger No 90 (1:50 000)

Parking Facilities

Legburthwaite car park (GR 318195). There is further parking at Swirls picnic area and car park (GR 317168) off the A591 where there is a small information centre. The walk could start and finish at (9). Also there is Station Coppice lay-by parking (GR 316170) where the walk could start and finish at (10).

Route Description

■ **1** Start from the car park entrance. Turn right on the B5322. Proceed for 600m.
■ **2** Fork left, off the road, just beyond the Youth Hostel on the left at a telephone kiosk in the hamlet of Legburthwaite. A lane turns left, signposted to Glenridding via Sticks Pass. Continue up it for 200m to where it bends left at a barn on the left.
■ **3** Go straight ahead, off the lane, over a ladder-stile adjacent to a wall sign to Sticks Pass. Go ahead, uphill, on a path over grassland, bending right. Pass over a stile adjacent to a field-gate.
■ **4** Turn left over a water channel. Pass through a wicket-gate signposted Sticks Pass at the top of the next rise. Turn right across a stone footbridge over Sty Beck Falls. Proceed ahead for 30m.
■ **5** Bear left, then right after another 30m at a permissive footpath sign to Grasmere via Swirls. Bear right up to a wall corner. Turn right along a wall on the right.
■ **6** Fork left on the higher path where the wall drops down right. Cross a gated footbridge over Fisherplace Gill Falls. Bear left up the bankside to a wall corner. Bear right along the wall on

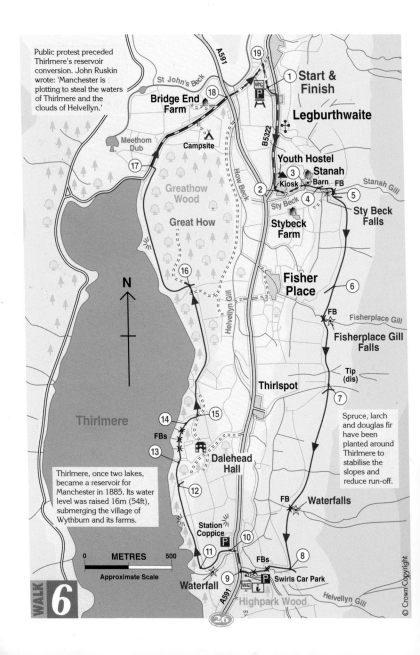

Public protest preceded
Thirlmere's reservoir
conversion. John Ruskin
wrote: 'Manchester is
plotting to steal the waters
of Thirlmere and the
clouds of Helvellyn.'

St John's Beck

A591

⑲

WC P

① **Start &
Finish**

Legburthwaite

B5322

**Bridge End
Farm**

⑱

Meetham
Dub

Campsite

⑰

How Beck

Youth Hostel
Stanah

③ Kiosk   Barn   FB

② ⑤

Sty Beck ④   **Sty Beck
Falls**

**Stybeck
Farm**

Stanah Gill

**Greathow
Wood**

Great How

⑯

Helvellyn Gill

**Fisher
Place**

⑥

FB   Fisherplace Gill

**Fisherplace Gill
Falls**

N

Tip
(dis)

Thirlspot

⑦

Spruce, larch
and douglas fir
have been
planted around
Thirlmere to
stabilise the
slopes and
reduce run-off.

⑭

⑮

FBs

⑬

**Dalehead
Hall**

⑫

Thirlmere

Thirlmere, once two lakes,
became a reservoir for
Manchester in 1885. Its water
level was raised 16m (54ft),
submerging the village of
Wythburn and its farms.

FB   **Waterfalls**

**Station
Coppice**

P

⑩

⑪

0   **METRES**   500

Approximate Scale

⑨   WC   i   P   **Swirls Car Park**

Waterfall

FBs   ⑧

A591

Highpark Wood

Helvellyn Gill

© Crown Copyright

WALK

6

㉖

the right.

■ **7** Ford a rivulet at a wall corner. Go straight across at cross-paths, as the wall drops away down right. Follow a former mining track over spoil heaps. It descends to cross a footbridge over a waterfall, as the wall leaves the path down right. Continue ahead downhill.

■ **8** Turn right at a junction at a wall corner on the right. Follow the path downhill. Cross a footbridge. Pass through a kissing-gate. Proceed through conifers to go through a wicket-gate. Turn left over a footbridge. Turn right to enter Swirls Car Park with an information centre and toilets. Go straight through the car park. Pass through a kissing-gate adjacent to a cattle-grid onto the A591.

■ **9** Turn right, along the road. Proceed for 130m. Turn left across the road. Go straight through Station Coppice lay-by car park. Descend steps.

■ **10** Go through the left of two facing kissing-gates, on a permissive path signposted to Legburthwaite and Great Howe. Bear right down a broad grassy path to a fence corner. Continue downhill with a waterfall and Helvellyn Gill gorge below on the left. Go through a kissing-gate. Pass through a gap in a wire fence, leaving the gorge.

■ **11** Go ahead along the eastern shore of Thirlmere on the fringes of the plantation. Pass through a gap in a broken wall.

■ **12** Fork left at a junction, off the main path, at a tree with a white waymarked sign attached. Go down through a gap in the broken wall ahead. Follow the lakeshore on the left for another 75m.

■ **13** Pass through a kissing-gate in a fence. Go through a broken wall. Cross

over three planked footbridges in succession, with Dalehead Hall up on the right.

■ **14** Bear right up a path, away from the lake, at a wall corner. Proceed along the wall on the left for 70m.

■ **15** Turn left through a kissing-gate at a low waymarked post. Continue on a broad path, uphill, bending right between trees. Follow the waymarks. Descend, bending left along a wall on the right. Pass through a kissing-gate and a broken wall. Bear right, uphill, bending left through mixed woodland.

A grassy descent to Thirlmere's eastern shore

■ **16** Turn left, downhill, at cross-paths. The path bends right to run parallel with the lakeshore down on the left. Descend with banister rails on the left. Pass through a kissing-gate. Go down steps onto the road.

■ **17** Turn right along the road for 600m, passing a campsite on the right to the A591.

■ **18** Cross the road. Pass through a kissing-gate adjacent to a field-gate. Follow a lane, with St John's Beck over to the left, for 250m.

■ **19** Turn right, through a kissing-gate, into the car park.

WALK 7

WREN CRAG - NADDLE FELL - ST JOHN'S IN THE VALE CHURCH
5.3 MILES (8.6 km)

Route Details

Distance	5.3 miles (8.6 km)
Degree of Difficulty	Moderate
Ascent	205m (672ft)
Time	3.5 hours

Start and Finish Points

Legburthwaite picnic area and car park (GR 318195) off the B5322.
From the junction at the village of Threlkeld on the A66 Penrith to Keswick road the start and finish point is situated 3.5 miles (5.6 km) south on the right, off the B5322.
From the hamlet of Legburthwaite, at the junction with the A591, the start and finish point is situated 650m north, on the left.

Maps Needed

OS Outdoor Leisure No 4 (1:25 000)
OS Outdoor Leisure No 5 (1:25 000)
OS Landranger No 90 (1:50 000)

Parking Facilities

Legburthwaite car park (GR 318195). There are no other suitable parking places adjacent to the route of this walk.

Route Description

■ **1** Start at the top end of the car park. Pass through a small gate. Turn left, along a walled lane with St John's Beck over to the right. Pass through a kissing-gate adjacent to a field-gate.

■ **2** Turn right along the A591. Cross the road bridge.

■ **3** Immediately turn right, off the road, over the stile at a footpath sign to St John's in the Vale and Bridge House. Immediately take a left fork. Proceed for only 20m.

■ **4** Bear left at another fork. Ascend a grassy path which bends left, then zig-zags to the summit of Wren Crag.

■ **5** Go ahead through a broken wall. Fork right up the rocky outcrop ahead. Continue along the Long Band ridge path with a small tarn below to the left towards the end of the ridge.

■ **6** Bear left at a cairn built round a low wooden post. Cross a stile over a wire fence. Follow down a broad grassy path bending right below Mart Crag up on the right. Skirt left round marshy ground.

■ **7** Filter right onto a path which descends to a wall junction ahead.

■ **8** Cross a ladder-stile at the wall junction. Follow a broad uphill path along a wall to the right.

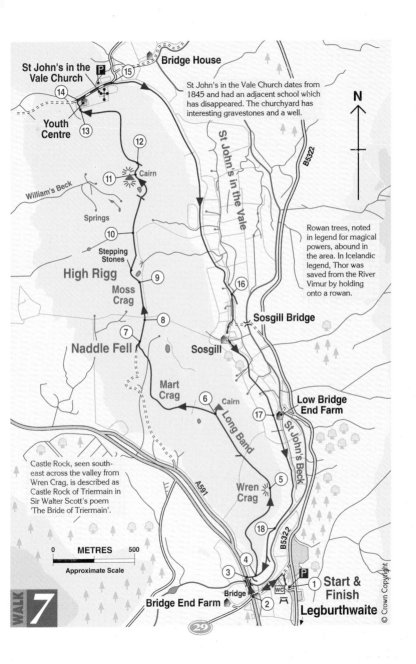

St John's in the Vale Church dates from 1845 and had an adjacent school which has disappeared. The churchyard has interesting gravestones and a well.

St John's in the Vale Church

St John's in the Vale Church

Bridge House

(15)

P

(14)

Youth Centre (13)

(12)

(11) Cairn

William's Beck

Springs

(10)

Stepping Stones

High Rigg

Moss Crag

(9)

(8)

Naddle Fell

(7)

N

Rowan trees, noted in legend for magical powers, abound in the area. In Icelandic legend, Thor was saved from the River Vimur by holding onto a rowan.

(16)

Sosgill Bridge

Sosgill

Mart Crag

(6) Cairn

Long Band

Low Bridge End Farm

(17)

St John's Beck

Castle Rock, seen south-east across the valley from Wren Crag, is described as Castle Rock of Triermain in Sir Walter Scott's poem 'The Bride of Triermain'.

(5)

Wren Crag

A591

(18)

B5322

0   METRES   500

Approximate Scale

(4)

(3)

Bridge

(2)

Bridge End Farm

(29)

WC

P

(1) **Start & Finish**

Legburthwaite

© Crown Copyright

WALK 7

St John's in the Vale Church below Naddle Fell

■ **9** Bend left away from the wall, below Moss Crag up on the left. Cross stepping-stones. Bear right to rejoin the wall on the right.

■ **10** Go straight ahead at the wall corner. Follow a broad grassy path towards a cairn on a summit ahead. Bear right over cross-paths up a short incline. Pass a small tarn on the left. Bend left to the summit cairn.

■ **11** Bear right from the cairn, down a rocky outcrop, to a pathway junction.

■ **12** Turn left down the fellside. Cross over a grassy plateau. Descend a path which swings left, then right.

■ **13** Pass through a kissing-gate at a wall. Go straight ahead to a telegraph pole. Bend left behind the Youth Centre and right on a narrow road.

■ **14** Turn right down the road, passing the Youth Centre and St John's in the Vale Church on the right. Proceed for another 130m.

■ **15** Turn right over a stile. Follow a broad path along a wall on the left, bending right, downhill. Cross three stiles adjacent to field-gates.

■ **16** Ignore the left branch down to Sosgill Bridge. Proceed ahead over a stile next to a gate. Pass a stone slab sign to Low Bridge End on the right. Ahead, cross a stile next to a gate, then through the kissing-gate. Cut through a plantation to emerge through another kissing-gate. Continue ahead.

■ **17** Pass behind and above Low Bridge End Farm on the left. The path ahead goes along a wall on the left. Cross a stile adjacent to a field-gate. Proceed along St John's Beck on the left.

■ **18** Bear right away from the beck, up through trees. Keep ahead on a terraced path, ignoring a left branch. Bend right, descending to (3). Follow the outward route back to the car park.

WALK 8

ST JOHN'S IN THE VALE CHURCH - TEWET TARN - CASTLERIGG STONE CIRCLE - NADDLE VALLEY
3.8 MILES (6 km)

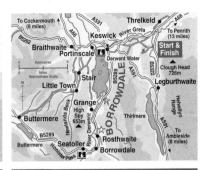

Route Details

Distance	3.8 miles (6 km)
Degree of Difficulty	Easy
Ascent	170m (557ft)
Time	3 hours

Start and Finish Points

Lay-by parking (GR 307225), opposite St John's in the Vale Church.
Turn south, off the A66, near Threlkeld onto the B5322 towards Thirlmere. Proceed for 1.2 miles (2 km). Turn right at the first right junction up a narrow gated road signed to St John's in the Vale Church and Carlisle Diocesan Youth Centre. The lay-by parking is 0.6 miles (1 km) on the right.

Maps Needed

OS Outdoor Leisure No 4 (1:25 000)
OS Landranger No 90 (1:50 000)

Parking Facilities

Lay-by parking (GR 307225).
There is also parking (GR 292237).
After visiting Castlerigg Stone Circle, turn right out of the gate. Go along the road for 150m to start the walk at (11).

Route Description

■ **1** Start left of the lay-by, opposite the church, at a footpath sign to Tewet Tarn. Cross a stile. Proceed ahead for 30m, fording a rivulet. Turn right on a path which bends left up open fell. Ford a rivulet. Take a left fork up to a wall ahead. Cross over a stile.

■ **2** Bear right with a grassy hillock on the right. Pick up a narrow path between grassy mounds. The path bends right, downhill. It levels out on reeded grassland.

■ **3** Bear right over pathless grassland, aiming to the right of Tewet Tarn. Cross a fence stile adjacent to a gate in a hollow. Go ahead over a small ridge, still aiming to the right of the tarn.

■ **4** Cross a stile with the foot of the tarn on the left. Go ahead for 100m to a signpost on a rocky outcrop.

■ **5** Turn right along the wall on the left. Follow the wall round left. Go through a field-gate.

■ **6** Bear right diagonally down a field onto a road.

■ **7** Turn left along the road. Proceed for 300m. Bear left at a junction. Go along the road for 250m. Bear left at the next junction. Cross Naddle Bridge. Proceed for another 40m.

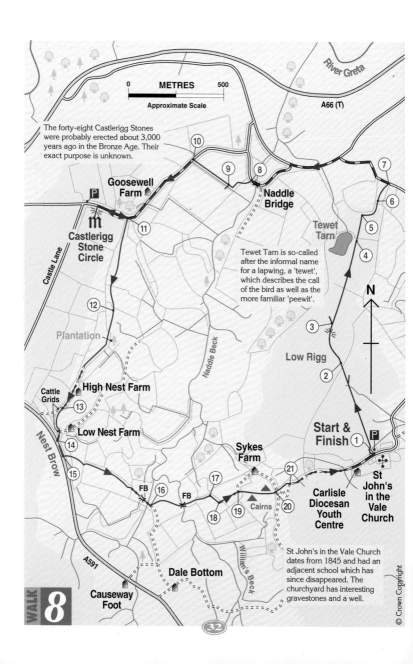

METRES

0 ——— 500

Approximate Scale

The forty-eight Castlerigg Stones were probably erected about 3,000 years ago in the Bronze Age. Their exact purpose is unknown.

River Greta

A66 (T)

Goosewell Farm

10
9 8
7
6
5

Naddle Bridge

Tewet Tarn

4

Castlerigg Stone Circle

11

Tewet Tarn is so-called after the informal name for a lapwing, a 'tewet', which describes the call of the bird as well as the more familiar 'peewit'.

Castle Lane

12

N

Plantation

Naddle Beck

3

Low Rigg

2

Cattle Grids

High Nest Farm

13

Low Nest Farm

14

Start & Finish 1

P

15

Nest Brow

FB 16 FB

17

Sykes Farm

21

St John's in the Vale Church

18 19 **Cairns** 20

Carlisle Diocesan Youth Centre

A591

Dale Bottom

William's Beck

St John's in the Vale Church dates from 1845 and had an adjacent school which has since disappeared. The churchyard has interesting gravestones and a well.

Causeway Foot

WALK **8**

32

© Crown Copyright

8 Turn left, off the road, over a stile adjacent to a field-gate at a footpath sign. Bear right across a field corner. Go over a ladder-stile. Bear left with a wall on the left.

9 Do not go through the field-gate ahead. Turn right at a wall sign to Castlerigg. Follow a permissive field path with a wall on the left. Pass over a stile in a wire fence onto the road.

10 Turn left along the road. Bend right, uphill, to a footpath sign to The Nest on the left.

11 Keep ahead along the road for 150m to Castlerigg Stone Circle on the left. Return to (11). Turn right through a field-gate at the footpath sign to The Nest. Descend ahead over grassland. Cross a ladder-stile. Go ahead across a field. Cross another ladder-stile.

12 Go ahead on a field path to a small plantation on the left at a wall corner. Cross over a stile. Continue with a hedge on the left, bending right, then left. Go through a gate. Pass High Nest Farm on the left. Follow a tarmac driveway ahead for 100m.

13 Pass through a gate to the left of a cattle-grid, leaving the driveway. Go ahead, bending left round the field boundary on the right. Cross a fence stile at the bottom of the field. Turn right on the Low Nest Farm driveway. Cross a cattle-grid and emerge onto the A591.

14 Turn left along the road at Nest Brow. Proceed for only 50m.

15 Turn left, off the road, through a wall gap at a footpath sign. Bear right down a grassy slope. Cross a stile in a wire fence and across a field. Pass over a stile. Bear left and go along a wall on the left, bending right, with now a fence on the left. Go down to the field corner. Pass through a field-gate onto a stony

cart-track. Go ahead over a footbridge. Proceed for 30m.

16 Turn left at a sign to St John's in the Vale Church. Cross grassland and go over a double-gated footbridge. Go ahead on a field path. Pass through a gateway. Proceed along the field fence on the left.

17 Turn right at a low waymarked post. Go along the path for 100m.

18 Turn left at a signpost to St John's in the Vale Church. Follow a field track for 100m.

Keswick's ancient Castlerigg Stone Circle

19 Fork right, off the track, at a left bend. Go through a gate between a wall and a fence. Ahead, go up a bankside with a cairn at the top on the right. Continue up a grassy slope, past a cairn on the left. Go through a kissing-gate at a footpath sign.

20 Cross Sykes Farm driveway. Ahead, go up a grassy bank, with the S-bend of an ascending track to the right. Emerge onto the track.

21 Bear left along the tarmac track. Go through a gateway and past Carlisle Diocesan Youth Centre on the right. Go ahead to the parking area.

WALK 9

KESWICK - GRETA GORGE - BRUNDHOLME WOOD - LATRIGG

6.4 MILES (10.4 km)

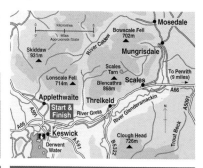

Route Details

Distance	6.4 miles (10.4 km)
Degree of Difficulty	Moderate
Ascent	308m (1010ft)
Time	4 hours

Start and Finish Points

Keswick Leisure Pool car park (GR 270238), adjacent to the former railway station. (fee payable at the Leisure Pool). From Keswick Tourist Information Centre in Moot Hall, go up Main Street for 100m. Turn left along Station Street, over crossroads, and along Station Road for 250m. On foot, go ahead, bearing right round the Leisure Pool. By car, turn right down Brundholme Road, bending left under a bridge, and left again to the Leisure Pool car park on the left.

Maps Needed

OS Outdoor Leisure No 4 (1:25 000)
OS Landranger No 90 (1:50 000)

Parking Facilities

Keswick Leisure Pool car park (GR 270238). The nearest alternative car park is in Victoria Street (GR 267235).

Route Description

■ **1** From the car park follow the dismantled railway track past the old railway station on the right. After 100m cross a bridge.

■ **2** Immediately turn left, off the track, down steps. Bear right on a road for only 15m.

■ **3** Turn right at a permissive footpath sign to Windebrowe. Pass over a bridge.

■ **4** Go ahead at a pathway junction, bending left along a fenced field on the left.

■ **5** Turn left onto a driveway at a footpath sign. Proceed for 40m.

■ **6** Turn right, along a road to Windebrowe. Proceed for180m.

■ **7** Fork right, off the road, at a footpath sign at the Riding Centre. Keep a large barn on the left to gain the far corner of a fenced equestrian exercise area. Turn left on a woodland path at a footpath sign to Brundholme Wood. Bend right down steps.

■ **8** Turn left along the River Greta on the right, passing under the A66 fly-over. The main path bears left, away from the river, up through Brundholme Wood.

■ **9** Fork right, following the sign to Latrigg and Blencathra and bending

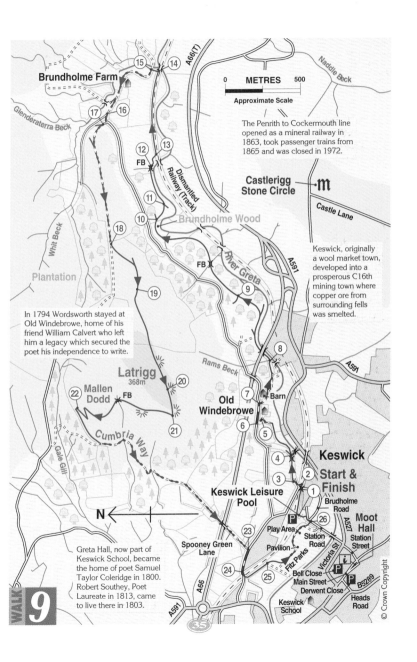

Brundholme Farm

Glenderaterra Beck

A66(T)

0 METRES 500

Approximate Scale

The Penrith to Cockermouth line opened as a mineral railway in 1863, took passenger trains from 1865 and was closed in 1972.

Castlerigg Stone Circle ♏

Castle Lane

Dismantled Railway (Track)

FB

Brundholme Wood

River Greta

Whit Beck

Plantation

FB

Keswick, originally a wool market town, developed into a prosperous C16th mining town where copper ore from surrounding fells was smelted.

In 1794 Wordsworth stayed at Old Windebrowe, home of his friend William Calvert who left him a legacy which secured the poet his independence to write.

A591

Rams Beck

Latrigg 368m

Mallen Dodd ✝ FB

Cumbria Way

Gale Gill

Old Windebrowe

Barn

A591

Keswick

Start & Finish

Brudholme Road

Moot Hall

Station Road

Station Street

A527

N ←

Keswick Leisure Pool

P

Play Area

Pavilion

Station Road

Fitz Parks

Spooney Green Lane

Bell Close

Main Street

Derwent Close

Keswick School

Victoria St

i

P

B5289

Heads Road

Greta Hall, now part of Keswick School, became the home of poet Samuel Taylor Coleridge in 1800. Robert Southey, Poet Laureate in 1813, came to live there in 1803.

A591

A66

35

© Crown Copyright

WALK 9

right along the terraced path. Cross a footbridge. Proceed ahead.

■ **10** Fork right where the river below describes a sharp arc, following a sign to the railway footpath, down steps.

■ **11** Turn left up the gorge with the river on the right. Cross a fence stile and pass over a footbridge.

The path on tiny Latrigg below mighty Skiddaw

■ **12** Bear right down the bankside and over a field. Cross a stile. Go up steps, with a railway bridge on the right.

■ **13** Turn left, along the dismantled railway track. Follow it for 550m.

■ **14** Turn left, off the track, just before a railway bridge at a sign to Keswick via Latrigg and Blencathra. Pass through a wicket-gate with Glenderaterra Beck on the right. Go up a wooden walkway and through a gate.

■ **15** Turn left on an uphill lane, bending right, then left past Brundholme Farm. Pass through a field-gate. Go ahead, past a right fork with a sign to Keswick. Proceed for 100m.

■ **16** Fork left, off the lane, with a wire fence on the left. Pass through a field-gate. Immediately, turn right over a stile adjacent to a gate at a sign to Skiddaw

and Underscar. Proceed for 10m.

■ **17** Fork left up the hillside. Bear right at the top on a rutted grassy path, bending left. Filter left up a broad ridge path. Pass through a field-gate at a plantation on the right.

■ **18** Bear diagonally left, off the path, up a grassy slope to a higher point on the ridge. Filter right, ascending a raised embankment.

■ **19** Bear left up the hillside before reaching a fence corner on the right. Pass over a fence stile adjacent to a gate. Go ahead on a ridge path up to the unmarked summit of Latrigg (368m/1207ft).

■ **20** Continue ahead on a raised path over a secondary summit. Go to the end of the ridge.

■ **21** Turn right down a broad grassy fellside path. Cross a planked footbridge. Ahead, the path bends, following an S-bend to the bottom.

■ **22** Turn left on a downhill path towards Keswick, passing through two kissing-gates and across a bridge over the A66. Continue down Spooney Green Lane to a road junction.

■ **23** Turn right along the road. Proceed for 150m.

■ **24** Turn left, opposite a buttress of a dismantled railway bridge on the right. Go through a gate. Turn left on a tarmac path. Go through a gate into Fitz Parks.

■ **25** Bear right, then left on the path with a wooded embankment on the left, past a cricket pavilion and then a play area on the right. Go up an embankment and through a kissing-gate.

■ **26** Turn left along the road. Proceed for 10m. Pass between bollards into the forecourt of Keswick Leisure Pool. Bear right, round the building to the car park.

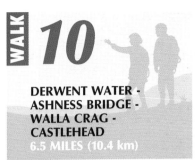

WALK 10

DERWENT WATER - ASHNESS BRIDGE - WALLA CRAG - CASTLEHEAD

6.5 MILES (10.4 km)

Route Details

Distance	6.5 miles (10.4 km)
Degree of Difficulty	Moderate
Ascent	361m (1183ft)
Time	4.5 hours

Start and Finish Points

Keswick Lakeshore car park (GR 266229) off Lake Road.
From Keswick information centre in Moot Hall, go down the Main Street for 100m. Turn left down Derwent Close to the junction. Turn left along the Heads Road. Proceed to the roundabout. Turn right down Lake Road for 200m to the car park on the left.

Maps Needed

OS Outdoor Leisure No 4 (1:25 000)
OS Landranger No 89 (1:50 000)
OS Landranger No 90 (1:50 000)

Parking Facilities

Keswick Lakeshore car park (GR 266229). There is further parking in the central car park (GR 265234) off Heads Road, and Bell Close car park (GR 267235) off Victoria Street.

Route Description

■ **1** Start at the car park exit. Turn left, along the lakeshore road, which becomes a broad path. Follow the sign to Friar's Crag ahead.

■ **2** Double back left from the wooded headland on a loop path. Descend steps. Turn right on a broad path. Pass through a wicket-gate. Fork right after 150m along the shoreline of Strandshag Bay. Cross two planked footbridges.

■ **3** Go through a wicket-gate. The path ahead skirts marshy woodland. Cross a footbridge. Bend right. Pass through a wicket-gate adjacent to a field-gate out of the wood.

■ **4** Turn right on a driveway which bends left. Pass a house, Stable Hills, on the right. Go through a wicket-gate adjacent to a cattle-grid. The path bends right, uphill.

■ **5** Bear left, off the driveway, at the top of the rise at a ground-level sign to Calfclose Bay. Bend left on the lakeshore path. Pass through a wicket-gate. Skirt round Calfclose Bay, bending right over a footbridge into woodland. Go ahead along the shoreline.

■ **6** Cross a footbridge over Cat Gill. Proceed along a shingle beach.

■ **7** Turn left up steps at a landing-

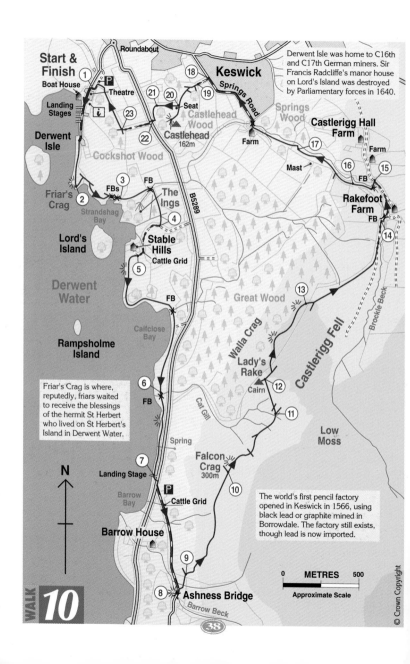

Start & Finish (1)
Boat House

Keswick

(18)

Springs Road

Derwent Isle was home to C16th and C17th German miners. Sir Francis Radcliffe's manor house on Lord's Island was destroyed by Parliamentary forces in 1640.

Theatre

Landing Stages

(21) (20) (19)

Seat

Springs Wood

Castlerigg Hall Farm

(23)

Castlehead Wood

Derwent Isle

Cockshot Wood

Castlehead 162m

Farm

(17)

Farm

(22)

Mast

(16) (15)

FB

FBs (3) FB

The Ings

Friar's Crag (2)

Rakefoot Farm

Strandshag Bay

B5289

(4)

FB

Lord's Island

Stable Hills

(14)

Cattle Grid

(5)

Derwent Water

FB

Calfclose Bay

Great Wood

(13)

Rampsholme Island

Walla Crag

Friar's Crag is where, reputedly, friars waited to receive the blessings of the hermit St Herbert who lived on St Herbert's Island in Derwent Water.

(6)

FB

Lady's Rake

Cairn (12)

Brockle Beck

Castlerigg Fell

(11)

Low Moss

Cat Gill

Spring

(7)

Landing Stage

Falcon Crag 300m

(10)

Barrow Bay

P

N

Cattle Grid

Barrow House

The world's first pencil factory opened in Keswick in 1566, using black lead or graphite mined in Borrowdale. The factory still exists, though lead is now imported.

(9)

0   **METRES**   500

(8) **Ashness Bridge**

Barrow Beck

Approximate Scale

© Crown Copyright

WALK 10

(38)

stage. Cross a high ladder-stile onto the B5289. Cross the road. Turn right up the minor road to Ashness Bridge and Watendlath. Pass through a wicket-gate adjacent to a cattle-grid. Proceed up the road to Ashness Bridge.

■ **8** Turn round. Proceed for 15m. Fork right, off the road. Go up a path to cross a high ladder-stile.

■ **9** Fork right up the fellside on a twisting path. Bear left at the top along the escarpment.

■ **10** Bear left at the top of the next rise down to Falcon Crag (300m/984ft). Return to (10). Turn left. Continue on the broad path, contouring left, round the three branches of Cat Gill.

■ **11** Bear left after the third branch up a grassy path.

■ **12** Turn right at a cairn in front of a wall. Proceed for 30m. Turn left over a stile at Lady's Rake. Bear up right and along the escarpment of Walla Crag.

■ **13** Leave the escarpment through a kissing-gate. Bear left, down Castlerigg Fell, with a wall on the left. Cross a stile adjacent to a field-gate near the bottom of the slope. Go ahead with a wall along on the left.

■ **14** Turn right across a footbridge over Brockle Beck at Rakefoot Farm. Turn left. Go down a lane, with the beck on the left for 200m.

■ **15** Double back left, off the lane. Turn right after 8m through a wicket-gate. Bend left down steps. Cross a footbridge. Turn right on a woodland path with the beck on the right.

■ **16** Bear right at a waymark sign. Pass through a kissing-gate. Go ahead with the gorge below on the right. Pass through a kissing-gate next to a stile. Go ahead, bending left downhill and past a radio mast on the left.

■ **17** Turn right into Springs Wood at the bottom. Proceed for 25m. Turn left down a broad path with a beck on the right. Pass through a kissing-gate adjacent to a field-gate into a farmyard. Go straight ahead between farm buildings. Pass through a field-gate. Cross a bridge. Follow Springs Road, downhill.

Distant Walla Crag looms over Derwent Water

■ **18** Turn left, off the road, onto a tarmac path at a low fence sign to Castlehead and Lake Road.

■ **19** Pass through a kissing-gate into Castlehead Wood. Go ahead on an uphill path, bending left.

■ **20** Bear left at a bench-seat, bending right up to the summit of Castlehead (162m/531ft). Return to (20). Turn left. Follow the path for 100m.

■ **21** Turn left down a path, bending left. Pass through a wall gap onto the B5289.

■ **22** Cross the road and go through a wall gap opposite. Bend left and immediately right down steps. Follow a gravelled path between fields. Pass through a gate into Cockshot Wood.

■ **23** Turn right at cross-paths. Proceed to the corner of the wood. Ahead, cross a stile into the car park.

DERWENT WATER - CAT BELLS - MANESTY PARK - BRANDELHOW PARK
5 MILES (8 km)

Route Details

Distance	5 miles (8 km)
Degree of Difficulty	Moderate
Ascent	380m (1246ft)
Time	3.5 hours

Start and Finish Points

Either: Keswick lakeside pay and display car park (GR 266229), off Lake Road, when taking a launch from Keswick pier, opposite the car park, to Hawes End jetty (GR 252229). **Or:** Gutherscale lay-by car park (GR 247212), on a lane off the minor road to Grange above the western shore of Derwent Water. Start and finish the walk 140m up the lane from (4).

Maps Needed

OS Outdoor Leisure No 4 (1:25 000)
OS Landranger No 90 (1:50 000)

Parking Facilities

Either: Keswick lakeside car park (GR 266229), when taking the launch. **Or:** Gutherscale car park (GR 247212). There are no other parking areas adjacent to this walk.

Route Description

■ **1** Start from the Hawes End jetty. Go ahead, up the shingled beach. Pass through a kissing-gate. Cross stone-slabs over a brook. Continue ahead uphill. Pass through a kissing-gate at the top of the rise. Bear right across a driveway.

■ **2** Go up the bankside opposite, through scattered trees. Bend right to filter left up a path along a wall on the right.

■ **3** Emerge onto a road at an S-bend. Go ahead, up the road. Pass through a wicket-gate adjacent to a cattle-grid. Follow the sign to Cat Bells and Yewthwaite up to a sharp left bend.

■ **4** Go up a short stony stairway, opposite the bend, where a sign indicates 'parking 150 yards' up a lane on the right. Turn left at the top at a pathway junction. Follow an ascending path, bending right and zig-zagging onto the ridge.

■ **5** Bear left up the ridge. Ascend over a series of rocky outcrops to the summit of Cat Bells (451m/1479ft).

■ **6** Go ahead, descending a band of rock. Continue on a grassy path down the ridge to cross-paths on the grassy saddle of Hause Gate.

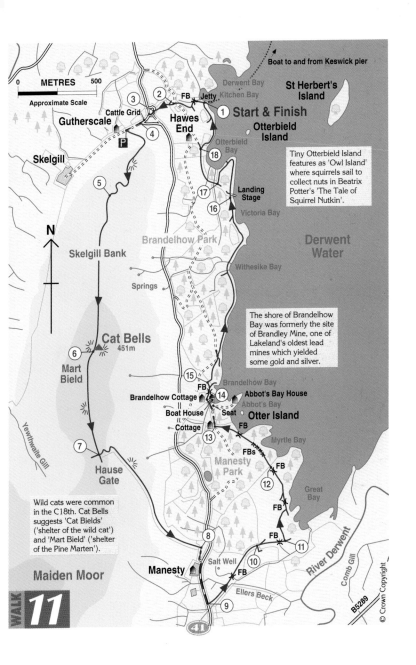

METRES 500

Approximate Scale

Boat to and from Keswick pier

Derwent Bay
Kitchen Bay
St Herbert's Island

FB Jetty
③ ②
Cattle Grid
Guntherscale
Hawes End
④
① Start & Finish
Otterbield Island

Skelgill
P

⑤
⑱
Otterbield Bay

Tiny Otterbield Island features as 'Owl Island' where squirrels sail to collect nuts in Beatrix Potter's 'The Tale of Squirrel Nutkin'.

N

Skelgill Bank

⑰
⑯
Landing Stage

Brandelhow Park

Victoria Bay

Derwent Water

Springs

Withesike Bay

Cat Bells
451m

Mart Bield

⑥

The shore of Brandelhow Bay was formerly the site of Brandley Mine, one of Lakeland's oldest lead mines which yielded some gold and silver.

Yewthwaite Gill

⑮ FB
Brandelhow Cottage
⑭
Abbot's Bay House
Brandelhow Bay
Abbot's Bay
Boat House
Seat
Otter Island
⑬
Cottage
FB
⑦

Hause Gate

Myrtle Bay
FBs
FB
⑫
FB

Great Bay

Wild cats were common in the C18th. Cat Bells suggests 'Cat Bields' ('shelter of the wild cat') and 'Mart Bield' ('shelter of the Pine Marten').

Manesty Park

⑧
FB
⑪
⑩

Maiden Moor

Salt Well
Manesty
FB
⑨
Ellers Beck

River Derwent

Comb Gill

B5289

© Crown Copyright

WALK
11

41

■ **7** Turn left, descending the fell on a twisting path which bends right along a fence on the right. Pass over a stile adjacent to a field-gate at the bottom.

■ **8** Continue ahead along a wall on the right to filter right onto a road. Proceed down the road for 250m past houses at the settlement of Manesty.

■ **9** Turn left, off the road, at a sign to Lodore. Pass through a wicket-gate adjacent to a field-gate. Bend left over reeded grassland with Ellers Beck to the right. Cross a footbridge. Continue ahead. Pass through a kissing-gate at a wall corner with a wood on the left. Proceed for 120m with a wall on the left and a fence on the right.

■ **10** Fork right, away from the wall, at the corner of a field fence on the right. Cross a single-plank causeway over marshy ground.

■ **11** Immediately turn left on a path, bending right round a rocky knoll up on the right. Filter left over stepping-stones at Derwent Water shore. Cross a long single-plank causeway. Bear up right, passing a wooded promontory to the right. Bend left over another single-plank causeway.

■ **12** Pass through a field-gate into Manesty Park. Continue ahead through woodland over four successive small footbridges. Pass another promontory on the right. Cross another footbridge. Continue on a broad shingly path, bending left through woodland.

■ **13** Turn right at a cottage ahead, with a fence corner and low-level sign to Brandelhow and Hawes End on the right. Pass through a field-gate. Ahead, fork left at a seat with the driveway to Abbot's Bay House on the right. Pass through a kissing-gate adjacent to a field-gate ahead.

■ **14** Bend right between a boathouse on the right and Brandelhow Cottage on the left. Skirt Brandelhow Bay. Cross a footbridge. Ahead, bear left up a broad path for 50m with a wall and wood on the right.

Cat Bells on the skyline over Derwent Water

■ **15** Turn right through a wicket-gate into the wood. Bear left down steps. Bear right at the bottom onto a lakeshore path. Keep to the shoreline of Brandelhow Park for 0.6 miles (1km).

■ **16** Pass through a kissing-gate adjacent to a field-gate with a landing-stage to the right. Emerge from woodland. Continue ahead at a left fork, on a loop path, skirting the lakeshore, round the promontory of Otterbield Bay. Follow a field-path, bending left along a wire fence and woodland on the right.

■ **17** Turn right onto a broad path. Proceed for 200m.

■ **18** Fork right, off the path, with an iron fence 70m ahead. Go down a bankside towards the lakeshore. Cross a stile. Follow the shoreline to Hawes End jetty to catch a return launch to Keswick. (Turn left, if returning to Gutherscale car park, following the route from (1) to (4). Go up the lane for 140m to the car park).

WALK 12

ST BEGA'S CHURCH - MIREHOUSE - BASSENTHWAITE LAKE - TENNYSON VIEWPOINT
3.5 MILES (5.7 km)

Route Details

Distance	3.5 miles (5.7 km)
Degree of Difficulty	Easy
Ascent	76m (249ft)
Time	2.5 hours

Start and Finish Points

Mirehouse car park (GR 235281) off the A591, adjacent to the Old Saw Mill Tea-Room where tickets, for a small charge, can be purchased to visit the grounds of Mirehouse and to follow a lakeside footpath around the Tennyson viewpoint beside Bassenthwaite Lake. Entrance to Mirehouse requires an extra fee.
From the roundabout on the A66, north of Keswick, take the A591 Carlisle road north-west. The car park is 3 miles (5 km) on the right in Dodd Wood.

Maps Needed

OS Outdoor Leisure No 4 (1:25 000)
OS Landranger No 90 (1:50 000)

Parking Facilities

Mirehouse car park (GR 235281). There are no other parking areas adjacent to this walk.

Route Description

■ **1** Start at the top left-hand corner of the car park. Turn left over a footbridge. Turn right up a short path. Turn left down a forest track for 50m.

■ **2** Fork right up a slope. Filter left, at the top, onto a broad forest path. Pass over Sandbeds Gill. Continue ahead on the narrowing downhill path, bending left down towards the road. Emerge onto the A591 at two stiles and a bridleway sign on the right.

■ **3** Turn right along the road. Proceed for 200m, passing the Ravenstone Hotel on the right and Ravenstone Lodge guest house on the left.

■ **4** Turn left to cross the road. Turn left at a footpath sign opposite. Go down steps. Bend right with Ravenstone Lodge on the left. Cross a stile adjacent to a field-gate. The field path follows along a hedge on the right for 40m, then bears left at a telegraph pole. Pass through a kissing-gate. Proceed ahead over a field.

■ **5** Cross a stile adjacent to a field-gate. Go ahead through a grove of trees to emerge through a kissing-gate. Continue ahead across the corner of the next field. Pass through a kissing-gate. Continue over another field. Go through

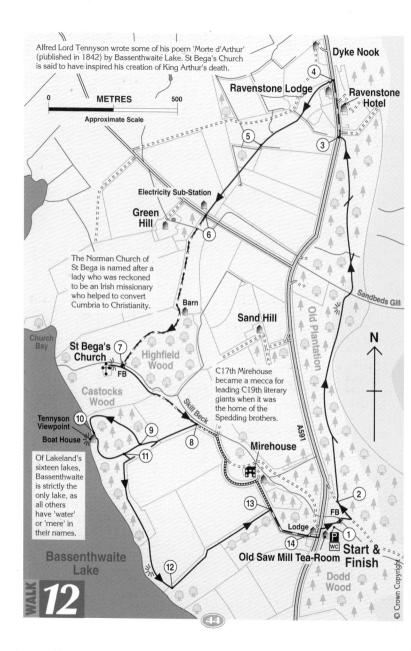

Alfred Lord Tennyson wrote some of his poem 'Morte d'Arthur' (published in 1842) by Bassenthwaite Lake. St Bega's Church is said to have inspired his creation of King Arthur's death.

Dyke Nook

Ravenstone Lodge

Ravenstone Hotel

0   METRES   500

Approximate Scale

Electricity Sub-Station

Green Hill

The Norman Church of St Bega is named after a lady who was reckoned to be an Irish missionary who helped to convert Cumbria to Christianity.

Barn

Sand Hill

Sandbeds Gill

Old Plantation

Church Bay

St Bega's Church

Highfield Wood

FB

Castocks Wood

C17th Mirehouse became a mecca for leading C19th literary giants when it was the home of the Spedding brothers.

Skill Beck

Tennyson Viewpoint

Boat House

Mirehouse

Of Lakeland's sixteen lakes, Bassenthwaite is the only lake, as all others have 'water' or 'mere' in their names.

A591

Lodge

FB

Old Saw Mill Tea-Room

Bassenthwaite Lake

Start & Finish

WC

Dodd Wood

© Crown Copyright

WALK 12

44

a kissing-gate into another field. Continue ahead to an electricity sub-station on the right. Go through a kissing-gate. Cross a minor road.

Skill Beck en route for Bassenthwaite Lake

■ **6** Go through the field-gate opposite at a footpath sign to St Bega's Church. Continue along the church driveway, bending left. Pass through a field-gate with a small barn on the left. The driveway descends, bending right and left. Cross a footbridge over Skill Beck.

■ **7** Immediately turn right. Proceed for 75m to St Bega's Church. Return to (7). Go ahead, past the footbridge on the left, on a path with Skill Beck on the left. Continue ahead over grassland to a field-gate.

■ **8** (Non ticket-holders go ahead through the gate and follow the driveway round Mirehouse to (13)). Ticket-holders do not go through the field-gate. Turn right at a sign to the lakeside. Follow a permissive path along a fence on the left. Pass through a wicket-gate adjacent to a field-gate into Castocks Wood. Proceed ahead as far as a low waymarked post.

■ **9** Turn right off the broad path. Follow a meandering woodland path down to the eastern shore of Bassenthwaite Lake. Turn left, along the shoreline, to a boathouse and the stone lectern at the Tennyson viewpoint.

■ **10** Continue ahead along the shore on a path which bends left, away from the lake, as far as a sign to the Old Saw Mill Tea-Room and car park.

■ **11** Turn right, following the sign, along a woodland path. Pass through a kissing-gate to emerge from the wood and rejoin the lakeshore on the right. Follow the waymarked field-path above the shore. Go through another kissing-gate.

■ **12** Immediately turn left at a low waymark. Follow the path, uphill, over grassland along a wire fence on the left. Go through a wicket-gate ahead at the field corner. Proceed through the wooded grounds of Mirehouse. Emerge through a field-gate onto the main driveway to Mirehouse.

St. Bega's Church on the shore of Bassenthwaite Lake

■ **13** Turn right along the driveway.

■ **14** Go ahead to a field gate adjacent to a lodge house. Pass through the field gate by the footpath sign onto the A591. Cross the road. Turn left along the road. Proceed for 50m. Turn right into the car park.

WALK 13

LODORE FALLS - WATENDLATH TARN - BRUND FELL - KING'S HOW

6 MILES (9.6 km)

Route Details

Distance	6 miles (9.6 km)
Degree of Difficulty	Moderate
Ascent	387m (1269ft)
Time	4.5 hours

Start and Finish Points

Double lay-by parking area (GR 256176), off the B5289 Borrowdale road, at the foot of Grange Crags. From the roundabout on the southern outskirts of Keswick, follow the B5289 south towards Borrowdale for 3.7 miles (6 km) to the lay-by car park, situated on the left.

Maps Needed

OS Outdoor Leisure No 4 (1:25 000)
OS Landranger No 90 (1:50 000)

Parking Facilities

Double lay-by parking area (GR 256176). There is limited parking at Watendlath (GR 276163), though access is not easy along a very narrow minor road often congested with traffic during the summer months. If used, start and finish the walk at (15).

Route Description

■ **1** Cross the B5289. Turn right on a roadside path. Proceed for 700m.

■ **2** Turn left, off the road, at a footpath sign. Go through a field-gate. Proceed with Comb Gill on the right. Pass over a stile adjacent to a field-gate.

■ **3** Turn right, over grassland. Pass over a stile. Go ahead with the River Derwent on the left for 200m.

■ **4** Turn right, away from the river, at a footbridge on the left. Proceed on a shaly path over reeded grassland. Pass through a field-gate.

■ **5** Turn left along the B5289. Proceed for 150m.

■ **6** Turn right across the road. Go up an unmarked driveway opposite, with the Lodore Swiss Hotel on the left. Bend left round the rear of the hotel. Follow a sign to the falls. Turn right, over a footbridge. Bend right, round a hummock on the right. Fork right on a short loop path to Lodore Falls.

■ **7** Continue ahead over cross-paths away from the Falls. Proceed up a woodland path, ignoring a left fork.

■ **8** Double back right, uphill, bending left along a ledge path at the base of a rock wall of Gowder Crag.

■ **9** Fork left at the top. Pass through a

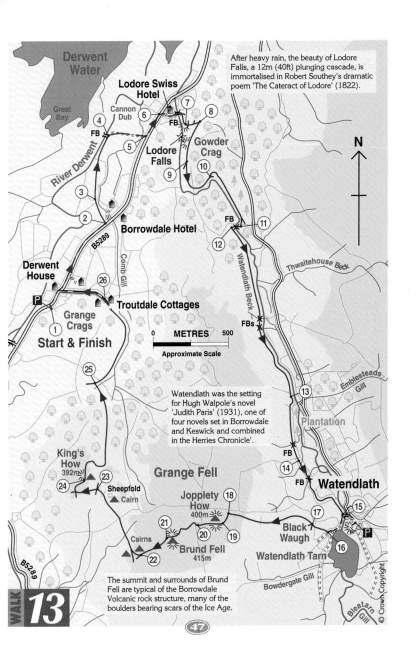

Derwent
Water

Great
Bay

Lodore Swiss
Hotel

After heavy rain, the beauty of Lodore Falls, a 12m (40ft) plunging cascade, is immortalised in Robert Southey's dramatic poem 'The Cateract of Lodore' (1822).

Cannon
Dub

(4)
FB
(5)
(6)
FB
(7)
(8)

N

River Derwent

(3)
(2)

Lodore
Falls
(9)

Gowder
Crag
(10)

B5289

Borrowdale Hotel

FB
(11)

(12)

Comb Gill

Watendlath Beck

Thwaitehouse Beck

Derwent
House

P

(26)

(1)
Grange
Crags

Troutdale Cottages

FBs

METRES   500
0

Approximate Scale

Start & Finish

(25)

Watendlath was the setting for Hugh Walpole's novel 'Judith Paris' (1931), one of four novels set in Borrowdale and Keswick and combined in the Herries Chronicle'.

(13)

Emblesteads
Gill

Plantation

King's
How
392m
(23)
(24)

Grange Fell

Sheepfold
Cairn

FB
(14)

FB

Watendlath

Jopplety
How
400m
(18)

(17)

(15)

B5289

(21)
Cairns
(22)
(20)
(19)

Brund Fell
415m

Black
Waugh

(16)

P

Watendlath Tarn

The summit and surrounds of Brund Fell are typical of the Borrowdale Volcanic rock structure, many of the boulders bearing scars of the Ice Age.

Bowdergate Gill

Bleatarn Gill

© Crown Copyright

WALK
13

wall gap. Contour left, round the hill, with Watendlath Beck down on the right.

■ **10** Keep left on the high path at a fork. The path bends right, downhill, over a depression. Bear right along the lower beckside path. Pass over a high ladder-stile out of the wood.

■ **11** Turn right at a footpath sign. Go along a wall on the right. Cross a footbridge over Watendlath Beck.

■ **12** Turn left, to Watendlath, marked on a ground-indicator. Follow the beck on the left. Pass over two footbridges after 600m. Cross another footbridge and later through a kissing-gate.

■ **13** Bear right up steps along a wall and small copse on the left. Bend left through a wicket-gate at the top. Continue along the wall on the left. Cross a footbridge. Go through a wicket-gate ahead.

■ **14** Ford a shallow brook ahead. Pass over a footbridge, then through a field-gate. Bend left, then right, away from the wall. Descend along the beck on the left. Go through a field-gate.

■ **15** Turn left, over a bridge, into the settlement of Watendlath. Return to point (15). Bear left along the beck. Pass through a kissing-gate adjacent to a field-gate. Bear right, uphill, at a signposted fork. Proceed for 50m.

■ **16** Turn right, off the path, at a wall and fence corner on the left. Cross a broken wall. Follow up a grassy path. Pass through a kissing-gate.

■ **17** Take the right of three paths. Go up a short rocky ascent. Follow a path with a wall over on the right. Pass over a broken wall on a marshy plateau, moving closer to the wall on the right.

■ **18** Turn left up a green path to the pointed pinnacle of Jopplety How (400m/1312ft) up on the right.

■ **19** Go ahead over a plateau between outcrops to a wall corner. Go along the wall on the right for 20m.

■ **20** Turn right over a ladder-stile. Bear left away from the wall, bending right and turning sharp left up a short steep slope. Bend round right to the summit of Brund Fell (415m/1361ft).

■ **21** Continue ahead along the ridge, before descending between outcrops.

■ **22** Fork right at the first cairn. Turn right downhill. Ford a shallow rivulet. Cross a ladder-stile. Go ahead, past a large cairn and sheepfold on the right. Drop down to cross a fence-stile.

■ **23** Go over cross-paths, bending left up a short steep rocky ascent. Turn sharp right at cross-paths over the rise, and up a winding path to the summit of King's How (392m/1286ft).

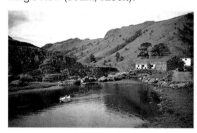

Watendlath Beck flowing from its lovely tarn

■ **24** Ahead, descend a rocky path, bending round right down a grassy rake. Bend left over a plateau round a rocky outcrop on the left. Descend a wooded gorge down a stepped path.

■ **25** Turn right at a wall ahead. Cross a stile. Turn left down the valley, along Comb Gill on the right. Cross a plateau away from the gill. Pass through a field-gate at Troutdale Cottages.

■ **26** Bend left down a lane. Emerge onto the B5289. Turn left along the road. Proceed for 120m to the parking lay-by.

WALK 14

SEATOLLER - CASTLE CRAG - RIVER DERWENT - JOHNNY WOOD
4 MILES (6.5 km)

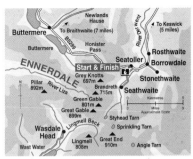

Route Details

Distance	4 miles (6.5 km)
Degree of Difficulty	Easy
Ascent	210m (689ft)
Time	3 hours

Start and Finish Points

Car park (GR 246138) in the village of Seatoller in Borrowdale, off the B5289 Keswick to Buttermere road.

Maps Needed

OS Outdoor Leisure No 4 (1:25 000)
OS Landranger No 90 (1:50 000)

Parking Facilities

Car park at Seatoller (GR 245138). Seatoller Barn is a Lake District National Park Information Centre, situated right out of the car park in the village.
There is also a car park (GR 257148), off the B5289, in Rosthwaite village. It is liable to be busy in the high season. From here, follow signposted field paths south to Peat Howe and over the bridge to begin at (14). Alternatively, follow the lane, west from Rosthwaite, and over New Bridge to begin the walk at (12).

Route Description

■ **1** Turn right from the car park entrance. Follow the B5289 for 200m through Seatoller.

■ **2** Turn right just before the road bends left at two large stone gate-pillars. Pass through a kissing-gate adjacent to a double field-gate. The ascending track passes through a field-gate, then bends sharp left. Pass through a kissing-gate adjacent to a field-gate. Go ahead on the track and over a stile adjacent to a field-gate. Proceed to a cairn.

■ **3** Fork right, off the track, up a grassy incline. Pass through a kissing-gate at the top of the rise at a junction of walls.

■ **4** Turn right along the wall on the right. Cross a gated footbridge over Scaleclose Gill. Keep ahead on a path along a wall on the right. Go through a broken wall.

■ **5** Pass over a footbridge and go through a wicket-gate ahead. Ford a shallow rivulet. Pass over cross-paths. Drop down left and cross a stile adjacent to a wicket-gate. Turn right over two footbridges spanning Tongue Gill.

■ **6** Ascend the bankside opposite. Follow the path ahead parallel to the wall down on the right. Drop down to

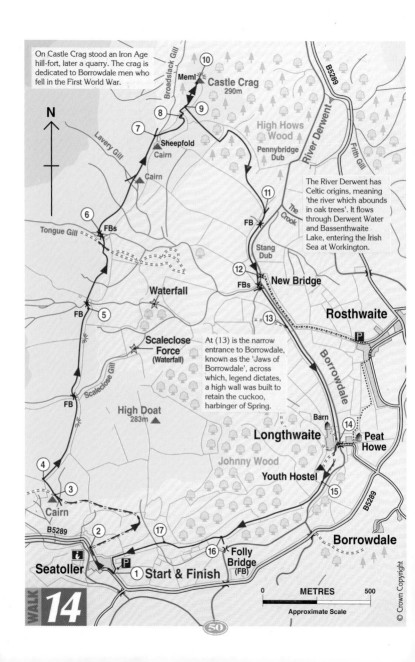

On Castle Crag stood an Iron Age hill-fort, later a quarry. The crag is dedicated to Borrowdale men who fell in the First World War.

N

Broadslack Gill

(10)

Meml

Castle Crag
290m

High Hows Wood

Pennybridge Dub

(8) (9)

(7)

Lavery Gill

Sheepfold

Cairn

Cairn

The River Derwent has Celtic origins, meaning 'the river which abounds in oak trees'. It flows through Derwent Water and Bassenthwaite Lake, entering the Irish Sea at Workington.

River Derwent

B5289

Frith Gill

(6)

FBs

(11)

FB

The Crook

Tongue Gill

Stang Dub

Waterfall

(12)

FBs

New Bridge

Rosthwaite

(5)

FB

P

Scaleclose Force
(Waterfall)

Scaleclose Gill

(13)

At (13) is the narrow entrance to Borrowdale, known as the 'Jaws of Borrowdale', across which, legend dictates, a high wall was built to retain the cuckoo, harbinger of Spring.

Borrowdale

FB

High Doat
283m

Barn

(14)

Longthwaite

Peat Howe

Johnny Wood

(4)

Youth Hostel

(3)

Cairn

(15)

B5289

B5289

(2)

(17)

Borrowdale

Seatoller

P

(1) **Start & Finish**

(16)

Folly Bridge
(FB)

0   **METRES**   500

Approximate Scale

© Crown Copyright

WALK 14

50

ford Lavery Gill. Filter right onto a former quarry track at a cairn at the top of the slope.

■ **7** Filter right, off the track, at the next cairn on the corner of a sheepfold. Go down a grassy bank. Cross a shallow depression. Go ahead, uphill, with a rock wall on the right to pass through a wall gap. Continue uphill along a wire fence on the right over a short grassy plateau. Bend left round a rocky outcrop on the left.

■ **8** Turn right over a stile in the wire fence. Immediately turn left over a ladder-stile. Bear right up the bankside.

■ **9** Keep ahead nearing the top of the bank with a ladder-stile above on the right. Cross a shaly plateau. Turn left to follow a steep zig-zagging path up a slate spoil-heap to the summit of Castle Crag (290m/951ft).

■ **10** Return to (9). Turn left over the ladder-stile. Descend ahead on a broad path over a grassy saddle. Go steeply down the fellside. Pass through a wicket-gate at the bottom to enter woodland. Turn left on a terraced path which bends right at spoil-heaps. Descend to emerge from woodland onto grassland. Pass over a stile adjacent to a field-gate at the bottom.

■ **11** Turn right onto a broad track through scattered trees. Pass over a stone-slab footbridge and follow the path along the River Derwent. Pass over a stile adjacent to a field-gate. Proceed for 80m.

■ **12** Keep ahead with the river on the left at a junction with the humpback New Bridge on the left. Cross a gated footbridge and over another footbridge. Continue along an embankment path.

■ **13** Pass through a wicket-gate. Continue on the permissive embankment path. Go through a

kissing-gate at a barn on the right. Filter onto a farm track after 12m. Proceed for 70m.

■ **14** Bear right through gates with a humpback bridge on the left. Go up the driveway of Longthwaite Youth Hostel. At a fork, follow the footpath sign to Seatoller. Pass in front of the hostel building. Proceed for 120m.

On the path to historic Castle Crag ahead

■ **15** Go through a kissing-gate into Johnny Wood. Follow the path along the river on the left. It narrows over rocks and exposed tree roots to pass through a kissing-gate. Go ahead uphill. Pass through a field-gate at the top of a slope. Ahead, go through a broken wall to a junction with Folly Bridge below on the left.

■ **16** Immediately turn right, along the broken wall on the right. Pass through a gap in a broken wall. Go through another gap in a broken wall. Bend up right at a 'no path' sign. Go through a kissing-gate at the top of the rise.

■ **17** Turn left, along a wall on the left. Ford a rivulet. Proceed for 150m. Turn left over a stile adjacent to a field-gate. Descend the bankside into the car park.

WALK 15

BUTTERMERE - BURTNESS WOOD - GATESGARTHDALE BECK - CRAG WOOD
4.5 MILES (7.2 km)

Route Details

Distance	4.5 miles (7.2 km)
Degree of Difficulty	Easy
Ascent	15m (49ft)
Time	2.5 hours

Start and Finish Points

Car parks in Buttermere village (GR 175169), off the B5289.

Maps Needed

OS Outdoor Leisure No 4 (1:25 000)
OS Landranger No 89 (1:50 000)
OS Landranger No 90 (1:50 000)

Parking Facilities

Apart from the car parks in Buttermere, there is one just out of the village, off the B5289 to Cockermouth.
There is also limited lay-by parking (GR 177171) near the church, up the hill from the village, on the junction of the B5289 and the minor road to Keswick.
Further parking (GR 196150) is available opposite Gatesgarth Farm, off the B5289. If using this, the walk could begin and finish at (8).

Route Description

■ **1** Start from the car park, going left of the Fish Hotel at a bridleway sign to Buttermere Lake/Scale Bridge. Follow a broad track bending left to pass through a kissing-gate adjacent to a field-gate.
■ **2** Pass a junction on the right to Scale Force/Scale Bridge. Bend right to pass through a field-gate. Go through a kissing-gate adjacent to a field-gate at the bottom of the track.
■ **3** Turn right on a path between wire fences. Cross a footbridge. Turn left along a wall on the right. Turn right through a field-gate.
■ **4** Turn left into Burtness Wood. Proceed for 100m. Fork left on a lakeshore loop path. Pass through a wall gap. Take a left fork, on another lakeshore loop path. Pass over a footbridge. Continue ahead.
■ **5** Go down over a footbridge. Pass through a kissing-gate ahead to emerge from the wood. Filter left onto a bridleway. Continue ahead, crossing a footbridge over Comb Beck.
■ **6** Turn left at a bridleway sign, immediately after a sheepfold on the left. Go through a kissing-gate adjacent to a field-gate. Cross a broad footbridge. Continue ahead on a straight track,

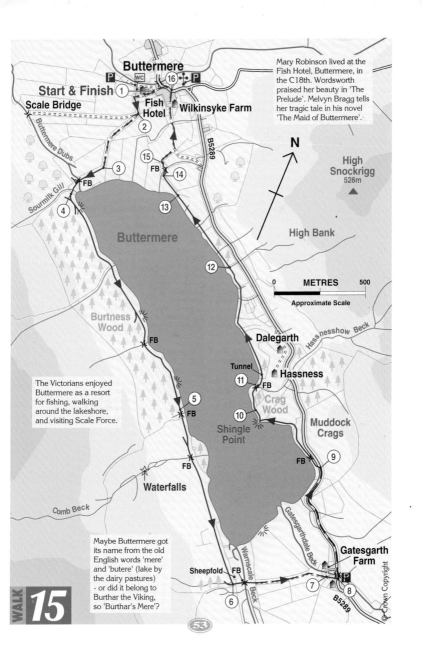

Buttermere

Start & Finish (1)

Scale Bridge

Fish Hotel

Wilkinsyke Farm

P · WC · (16) · P

Mary Robinson lived at the Fish Hotel, Buttermere, in the C18th. Wordsworth praised her beauty in 'The Prelude'. Melvyn Bragg tells her tragic tale in his novel 'The Maid of Buttermere'.

Buttermere Dubs

(2)

(3)

(15)

FB (14)

Sourmilk Gill

FB

(4)

(13)

N

High Snockrigg 526m

B5289

Buttermere

High Bank

(12)

0   **METRES**   500

Approximate Scale

Burtness Wood

FB

Hass nesshow Beck

Dalegarth

The Victorians enjoyed Buttermere as a resort for fishing, walking around the lakeshore, and visiting Scale Force.

Tunnel

(11) FB

Hassness

(5)

FB

(10)

Crag Wood

Shingle Point

Muddock Crags

FB

FB (9)

Waterfalls

Comb Beck

Gatesgarthdale Beck

Maybe Buttermere got its name from the old English words 'mere' and 'butere' (lake by the dairy pastures) - or did it belong to Burthar the Viking, so 'Burthar's Mere'?

Sheepfold FB

Warnscale Beck

(6)

(7)

Gatesgarth Farm

P

(8)

B5289

© Crown Copyright

Across Buttermere to distant Fleetwith Pike

cutting across meadows. Pass through a kissing-gate adjacent to a field-gate. Go ahead to pass through another kissing-gate adjacent to a field-gate at Gatesgarth Farm.

■ **7** Proceed with a wire fence on the left along Gatesgarthdale Beck, with the farmyard over on the right. Emerge through a wicket-gate onto the road.

■ **8** Turn left on the road over the bridge. Proceed for 500m down to the lakeshore.

■ **9** Bear left, off the road, at a ground-level sign to Buttermere via lakeshore on a permissive path. Pass over a double-planked footbridge. Go through a kissing-gate in a wire fence. Pass through a wall gap. Follow the lakeshore path left over meadowland.

■ **10** Pass through a wicket-gate adjacent to a field-gate at Shingle Point. Bend right round the promontory. Cross a footbridge over Hassnesshow Beck.

■ **11** Bear right through a kissing-gate. Cross a pebbly beach to ascend into woodland. Go through a kissing-gate onto a wooded terraced lakeshore path.

Pass through a tunnel hewn out of the rock. Go through a kissing-gate. Continue ahead through parkland, after emerging from the wood.

■ **12** Pass through a kissing-gate into more woodland. Go through a field-gate. Proceed on the terraced lakeshore path.

■ **13** Pass through a kissing-gate at the foot of the lake. Go ahead to emerge from the trees through a kissing-gate. Continue on the path.

■ **14** Turn right. After 10m, turn left over a stone-slab footbridge. Go ahead between a wire fence and a wall. The path bends left, then right uphill, at a ground-level sign to Buttermere.

■ **15** Pass through a wicket-gate at the top of the rise. Follow a low-level sign to Buttermere. Turn left at a junction. Pass over a stile adjacent to a field-gate into the yard of Wilkinsyke Farm. Pass through three field-gates in the farmyard. Emerge onto the B5289.

■ **16** Turn left down the road. Proceed for 75m. Bear left, off the road, into Buttermere village.

WALK 16

RANNERDALE - BUTTERMERE VILLAGE - LONG HOW WOOD - CRUMMOCK WATER
5.7 MILES (9.2 km)

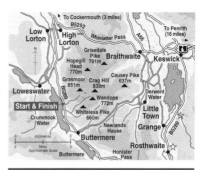

Route Details

Distance	5.7 miles (9.2 km)
Degree of Difficulty	Moderate
Ascent	220m (722ft)
Time	3.5 hours

Start and Finish Points

Two small roadside parking areas on the B5289 Cockermouth to Buttermere road at Cinderdale Common (GR 163194 and GR 163193), opposite the eastern shore of Crummock Water.

From Keswick, take the B5289 south into Borrowdale, over Honister Pass, and along the shores of Buttermere and Crummock Water. A return route to Keswick leaves Buttermere village on a narrow road over Newlands Hause.

Maps Needed

OS Outdoor Leisure No 4 (1:25 000)
OS Landranger No 89 (1:50 000)

Parking Facilities

As well as Cinderdale Common, there are car parks in and around the village of Buttermere (GR 175169) off the B5289. Start and finish the walk at (6).

Route Description

■ **1** Start from the rear of the parking area, going away from the lake. Follow Cinderdale Beck on the right for 50m. Turn right, fording the beck. Proceed on a broad path, parallel to a wall over on the right. Cross over a stile adjacent to a field-gate. Continue on the broad grassy path.

■ **2** Turn right, off the path, at a ground-level footpath sign. Go down to the beck. Cross a footbridge. Pass through a gate ahead.

■ **3** Turn left along a wall and Squat Beck on the left. Leave the wall at a corner on the left, going straight ahead up the valley. Ford a branch of Rowantree Beck. Bear right, uphill, with the beck on the right to a cairn marking the col at the head of Rannerdale.

■ **4** Turn right, on a broad path, descending the fellside towards Buttermere village below. Keep straight ahead over criss-cross paths. Bear left, down to a wall on reaching a plateau just above the village. Turn right with the wall on the left. Pass through a wicket-gate. Emerge onto the B5289.

■ **5** Cross the road. Turn left, downhill. Proceed for 300m. Turn right immediately after the Bridge Hotel into

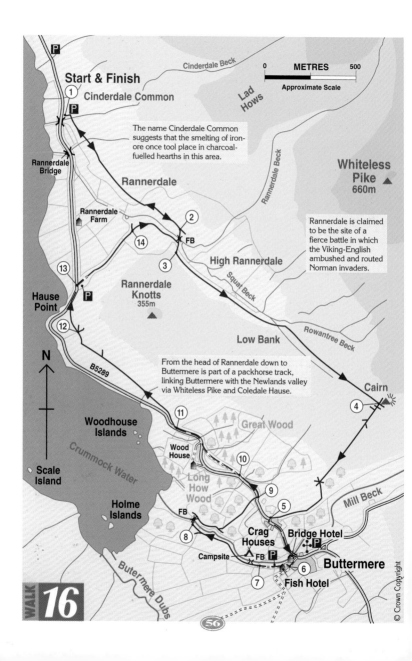

Start & Finish
Cinderdale Common
①
Cinderdale Common

The name Cinderdale Common suggests that the smelting of iron-ore once took place in charcoal-fuelled hearths in this area.

Cinderdale Beck

Lad Hows

Rannerdale Beck

Whiteless Pike ▲ 660m

Rannerdale Bridge

Rannerdale

Rannerdale Farm

②

⑭

FB

③

High Rannerdale

Rannerdale is claimed to be the site of a fierce battle in which the Viking-English ambushed and routed Norman invaders.

Rannerdale Knotts 355m ▲

Squat Beck

⑬

Hause Point
P

⑫

Low Bank

Rowantree Beck

N

B5289

From the head of Rannerdale down to Buttermere is part of a packhorse track, linking Buttermere with the Newlands valley via Whiteless Pike and Coledale Hause.

Cairn ④

Woodhouse Islands

Crummock Water

⑪

Great Wood

Wood House

⑩

Scale Island

Long How Wood

⑨

⑤

Holme Islands

FB

⑧

Mill Beck

Crag Houses

Bridge Hotel
P

Campsite

FB
P

⑥

Buttermere

Buttermere Dubs

⑦

Fish Hotel

METRES 0 — 500
Approximate Scale

WALK 16

56

© Crown Copyright

Buttermere village.

■ **6** Follow the sign to Crummock Water on the front of the Fish Hotel. Take the track to the right of the hotel with the car park and Mill Beck to the right.

Rannerdale Knotts viewed across Crummock Water

■ **7** Go through a kissing-gate at a footpath sign at the top right-hand corner of the car park. Follow the beck on the right with a campsite on the opposite bank. Pass a footbridge on the right. Continue along the beck. Go through a wicket-gate into a field. Proceed ahead.

■ **8** Cross a stile on the right with a sign to Buttermere village via Long How Wood. Pass over the footbridge. Turn right, doubling back upstream with the beck on the right. The path leaves the beck after 100m, climbing uphill into Long How Wood. Pass through a broken wall, then through a kissing-gate adjacent to a field-gate at the top of the rise. Emerge from the wood through a kissing-gate adjacent to a field-gate onto the B5289.

■ **9** Cross the road. Turn left. Proceed for 100m.

■ **10** Fork right, off the main road, onto the old road. Follow the loop path through woodland to rejoin the main road. Proceed for another 150m.

■ **11** Branch right, off the road, at a wall corner on the right. Follow the path up the bankside. The undulating terraced path contours round the fell with the road and Crummock Water below on the left. Fork left at the first rocky outcrop.

■ **12** Take the left of three forks at the next rocky outcrop. Go downhill towards the lakeshore to join the B5289 at the bottom. Turn right along the road. Proceed for 70m.

■ **13** Turn right, off the road, leaving the lake. Go through a small parking area with a National Trust sign to Rannerdale. Follow a path along a wall on the left with a rock wall on the right. Pass through a kissing-gate. Proceed for 70m.

Crummock Water seen from below Rannerdale Knotts

■ **14** Fork right, uphill, away from the wall. Join the beck on the left. Bear left down to the beck at a wall corner. Cross the footbridge. Bear left up to (2). Turn left and follow the outward route back to the parking area.

WALK 17

LOWESWATER - MAGGIE'S BRIDGE - HOLME WOOD - HUDSON PLACE
3.5 MILES (5.7 km)

Route Details

Distance	3.5 miles (5.7 km)
Degree of Difficulty	Easy
Ascent	60m (197ft)
Time	2 hours

Start and Finish Points

One of two lay-by parking areas (GR 118225) with a telephone kiosk, and (GR 122223), situated on the lakeside road at the northern corner of Loweswater Lake.
From Cockermouth, take the A5086 south, turning left on a minor road through Mockerin and Waterend.
From Keswick, the quickest route is the B5292 over Whinlatter Pass.

Maps Needed

OS Outdoor Leisure No 4 (1:25 000)
OS Landranger No 89 (1:50 000)

Parking Facilities

As well as the lay-by parking, there is a car park (GR134210) near Maggie's Bridge. Turn left (at (4)) off the minor road, towards Watergate Farm. Start and finish the walk at (5).

Route Description

■ **1** Start from the lay-by (GR 118225) with a telephone-kiosk. Turn right, along the road, running parallel to the eastern shore of Loweswater. Pass the second lay-by (GR 122223) on the right. Proceed for another 200m.

■ **2** Turn right, off the road, at a wall corner. Descend a stony path to the lakeshore. Turn left. Follow a wooded path along the lakeshore. Bear left up a path near the end of the woodland. Follow a stream and a wall on the right. Go through a field-gate to rejoin the road.

■ **3** Turn right uphill. Proceed for 800m as far as an ornate stone gateway at the entrance to the driveway up to Highcross on the left. Proceed for another 200m.

■ **4** Turn right at a bridleway sign. Follow a tarmac lane, bending back towards the lake head.

■ **5** Fork right at Maggie's Bridge with a small car park to the right. Follow the National Trust sign to Loweswater. Pass through a small gate adjacent to a field-gate with a sign to Watergate Farm, and Holmewood Bothy. The broad track crosses a concrete bridge over Dub Beck. It bends left to run parallel with the

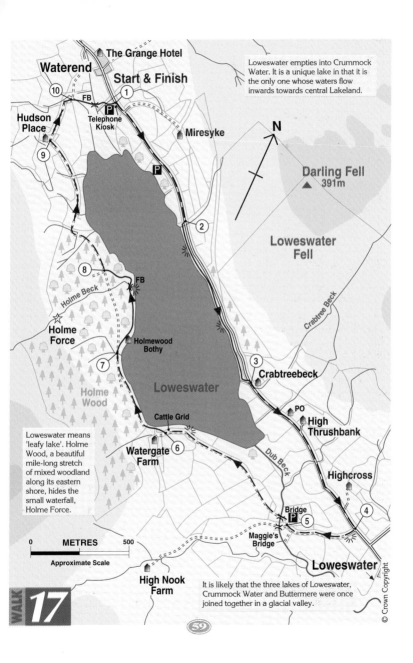

The Grange Hotel

Waterend

Start & Finish

⑩

FB

Hudson
Place

⑨

Telephone
Kiosk

P

Miresyke

P

②

N

Darling Fell
▲ 391m

Loweswater
Fell

Crabtree Beck

Loweswater empties into Crummock Water. It is a unique lake in that it is the only one whose waters flow inwards towards central Lakeland.

Holme Beck

⑧

FB

☆

Holme
Force

Holmewood
Bothy

⑦

Holme
Wood

Loweswater

③

Crabtreebeck

PO

High
Thrushbank

Cattle Grid

Watergate
Farm

⑥

Dub Beck

Highcross

Loweswater means 'leafy lake'. Holme Wood, a beautiful mile-long stretch of mixed woodland along its eastern shore, hides the small waterfall, Holme Force.

Bridge

P

⑤

④

Maggie's
Bridge

Loweswater

0   METRES   500

Approximate Scale

High Nook
Farm

It is likely that the three lakes of Loweswater, Crummock Water and Buttermere were once joined together in a glacial valley.

© Crown Copyright

WALK

17

The lovely sylvan shores of peaceful Loweswater

southern end of Loweswater. Go through a field-gate adjacent to a cattle-grid.

■ **6** Fork right, leaving the track, on approaching the farmyard of Watergate Farm on the left. Follow a broad grassy track. Aim for a small gate adjacent to a field-gate, with a short wall to the right bordering a wood and leading down to the lakeside. Pass through the gate. Follow a woodland path, running parallel to the lakeshore on the right.

■ **7** Turn right after fording a shallow stream, temporarily leaving the main path. Pass Holmewood Bothy on the right. The loop path continues to follow the shoreline round a wooded promontory. Cross over a footbridge. The path bends left, then right to rejoin the main woodland path.

■ **8** Turn right. The path bends right to pass over a stile adjacent to a field-gate. Proceed ahead across another stile adjacent to a field-gate. Continue up the walled path, bending left, away from the head of the lake. Climbing gradually, the path leads up to Hudson Place Farm.

■ **9** Turn right with the farm on the left. Pass through a field-gate. Descend the farm driveway which bends right, then left.

■ **10** Turn right at the left bend over a stile adjacent to a field-gate. Bear right over reeded grassland. Pass over a short wooden causeway across marshy ground. Cross a stile and another causeway. Bear right over another stile. Cross a small planked footbridge. Turn left along a hedge and ditch on the left. Pass through a wicket-gate adjacent to a field-gate onto the road. Turn right into the lay-by parking area.

WALK 18

ENNERDALE WATER - RIVER LIZA - ANGLER'S CRAG - RIVER EHEN

7 MILES (11.5 km)

Route Details

Distance	7 miles (11.5 km)
Degree of Difficulty	Moderate
Ascent	130m (426ft)
Time	4 hours

Start and Finish Points

A Forestry Commission car park (GR 110153) at Bowness Knott on the northern shore of Ennerdale Water. In the vicinity of Cleator Moor, turn east, off the A5086 onto one of the minor roads signposted to Ennerdale Bridge. Take the road east towards Croasdale. Pass the left turn to Croasdale. Turn right at the T-junction to Bowness Knott car park.

Maps Needed

OS Outdoor Leisure No 4 (1:25 000)
OS Landranger No 89 (1:50 000)

Parking Facilities

Apart from Bowness Knott, there is parking at (GR 094161), (GR 088156) and (GR 085154), adjacent to the walk route. Start and finish between points (13) and (15).

Route Description

■ **1** Start from the car park entrance. Cross the road. Go ahead up a grassy path to the top of a rocky outcrop for a viewpoint over Ennerdale Water.

■ **2** Continue ahead from the summit. Descend to the lakeshore.

■ **3** Turn left on the lakeshore path.

■ **4** Filter right on a tree-fringed forest track with which the lakeshore path has merged.

■ **5** Bear right, off the road, at a waymarked sign on the right indicating the Nine Becks Walk/Liza Path, just 30m before a junction from the left. The path leads down to the lakeshore over a grassy promontory with scattered trees and picnic tables. Keep to the shoreline. Veer right through a wall gap. At the head of the lake, the path runs along the River Liza on the right. (Keep on the track if the water level is high).

■ **6** Turn right at the end of the path at a junction with the track. Cross a footbridge (could be inaccessible when river is in flood). Go ahead on a grassland track with a wall to the right.

■ **7** Turn right over a waymarked ladder-stile before a field-gate ahead. Continue ahead along a wall fringing a plantation on the left. Turn left at a wall

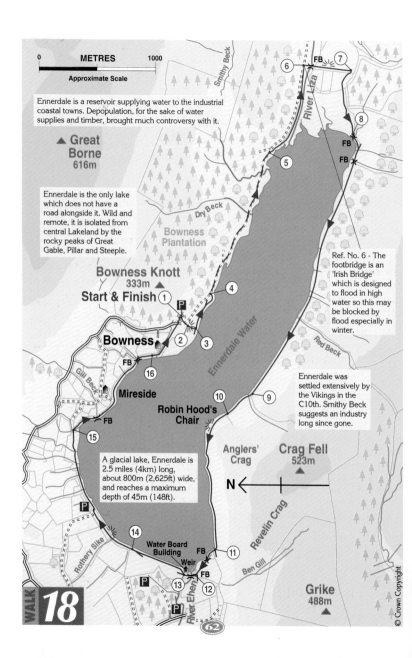

METRES

0 — 1000

Approximate Scale

Ennerdale is a reservoir supplying water to the industrial coastal towns. Depopulation, for the sake of water supplies and timber, brought much controversy with it.

▲ **Great Borne**
616m

Ennerdale is the only lake which does not have a road alongside it. Wild and remote, it is isolated from central Lakeland by the rocky peaks of Great Gable, Pillar and Steeple.

Smithy Beck

River Liza

Dry Beck

Bowness Plantation

Bowness Knott
333m ▲
Start & Finish ①
Ⓟ

Bowness
②
③
FB ⚓
⑯

Gill Beck

Mireside

FB ⚓
⑮

Robin Hood's Chair
⑩

Ennerdale Water

④

⑤

⑥ FB ⚓ ⑦

⑧
FB ⚓

FB ⚓

Ref. No. 6 - The footbridge is an 'Irish Bridge' which is designed to flood in high water so this may be blocked by flood especially in winter.

Red Beck

⑨

Ennerdale was settled extensively by the Vikings in the C10th. Smithy Beck suggests an industry long since gone.

Anglers' Crag

Crag Fell
523m ▲

N ←———

A glacial lake, Ennerdale is 2.5 miles (4km) long, about 800m (2,625ft) wide, and reaches a maximum depth of 45m (148ft).

Ⓟ

Rothery Sike

⑭

Water Board Building

FB ⚓ ⑪

Revelin Crag

Ben Gill

Ⓟ

Weir
⑬ ⑫
FB ⚓
Ⓟ

River Ehen

Grike
488m ▲

WALK **18**

Peace reigns over tranquil Ennerdale Water

corner. Pass over a stile adjacent to a field-gate. Continue ahead over reeded grassland.

■ **8** Pass over a footbridge on rejoining the wall on the left. Go through a field-gate. Keep ahead on the shore path, passing over a concealed stile left of a field-gate. Ford two rivulets. Go through a broken wall to cross a footbridge. The lakeshore path continues to meander through woodland.

■ **9** Cross a stile, having emerged from woodland. Ford a shallow stream. Continue along the shoreline.

■ **10** Pass through a broken wall. Gradually ascend Anglers Rock topping the rocky promontory of Robin Hood's Chair ahead. The path traverses a scree slope to climb a short rock step. Keep to the left on crossing this rocky outcrop. Descend another rock step to follow a path back down to the lakeshore. Continue along the shore.

■ **11** Pass through a kissing-gate on approaching the foot of the lake. Cross a footbridge to continue along the shore.

■ **12** Pass to the left of a weir. Turn right over a broad footbridge across the River Ehen on the right. Pass through a kissing-gate adjacent to a field-gate. Proceed for 35m.

■ **13** Turn right off the main path. Follow a narrow loop path through reeds to return to the lakeshore. Turn left along the shoreline, briefly leaving it to skirt left round clumps of gorse. Rejoin the main path.

■ **14** Go through a field-gate with the lake to the right. Ford Rothery Sike. Pass through a kissing-gate adjacent to a field-gate. Continue ahead along the shoreline. Pass a car park on the left. Go through a kissing-gate adjacent to a field-gate. The path now temporarily leaves the lakeshore. Cross a stile adjacent to a field-gate.

■ **15** Turn right down a broad path along a stream on the right. Turn left along the lakeshore path, bending right around a bay. Ahead, pass over two footbridges. Proceed for another 175m.

■ **16** Go over a stile adjacent to a wicket-gate. Immediately bend left, uphill, away from the shoreline between walls. Pass through a gated wall gap. Go ahead on an ascending path. Pass through a gap in the walls. Cross the forest road ahead. Enter the car park.

Walking & Safety Tips

This section is virtually the same as we publish in our Classic Walks of Discovery Series which are designed for the very serious walker, covering much longer routes on very difficult and high altitude terrain. However, the basic principles still apply so we have retained this detail for your information.

It is absolutely essential that anyone venturing out into the countryside, particularly hilly terrain, be correctly prepared to reduce the risk of injury or fatality. No amount of advice could cover all possible situations that may arise. Therefore the following walking and safety tips are not intended to be an exhaustive list, but merely a contribution from our personal experiences for your consideration.

Clothing & Equipment

The lists represent the basic equipment required to enjoy a full day's hill walking, reasonably safely and comfortably.

CLOTHING:- Strong, sensible footwear, preferably boots with a good sole, but strong trainers or lightweight boots can be worn during prolonged dry weather; warm shirt, fibre pile jacket, warm woollen sweater, windproof and waterproof hooded anorak and overtrousers (several thin layers insulate more adequately than one layer), thermal gloves; woollen hat or balaclava, warm trousers (avoid denim/jeans which become very clammy and cold when wet and could induce exposure), and good quality woollen socks or stockings, protected by waterproof gaiters.

EQUIPMENT:- Good compass and maps of the areas, along with a survival bag, whistle or torch for implementing the International Distress Signal - 6 long blasts/flashes in quick succession followed by one minute pause then repeated (the answering signal is 3 blasts or flashes). A basic first-aid kit should also be carried, which contains - bandages, sticking plasters, safety pins, scissors and some gauze pads. Take a rucksack in which to carry your equipment, and some food, plus extra food for emergency rations - chocolate, fruit cake, cheese and dried fruit. Extra liquid should be carried in hot weather.

Preparation & Procedure

Ensure that yourself and the others are adequately equipped and that no-one is overburdened. Learn how to use your map and compass competently. You should always be able to at least locate yourself on a map. Find out the weather forecasts for the area. Always consider the wind chill factor - even the gentlest of winds can reduce effective temperatures to a dangerous level. Plan both the route and possible escape routes beforehand, balancing terrain, weather forecast and the hours of daylight against experience whilst allowing for a safety margin. Always try to plan your walk so the prevailing wind is behind you. Always try to walk in company. It is safer and more enjoyable. Gain a basic understanding of first aid. Try to leave written details of your route, point of departure, number in your group, destination and estimated time of return. In an emergency this information could save a life. Maintain a steady rhythm, at the pace of the slowest walker. Take care when you are walking to avoid sprains. Be very careful where you step and remain extremely vigilant about avoiding the adder, Britain's native poisonous snake. Take regular breaks - mainly to check your progress and the next stage. Keep an eye on the weather. Always be prepared to turn back if necessary. On completion of your journey, inform the person with whom you left your written information of your safe arrival.

Stay Wise - Stay Alive

First aid on the hills requires both knowledge and common sense. If in doubt concentrate on the comfort and morale of the casualty. **IN AN EMERGENCY: STOP AND THINK - DO NOT PANIC**. If you are lost - check your surroundings carefully and try and locate yourself on your map. Find shelter and decide whether it is safe or best to use an escape route. If someone is injured, or is showing the signs of exposure (i.e. stumbling and slurred speech, shivering, irrational behaviour or collapse and unconsciousness) **STOP IMMEDIATELY**, prevent further heat loss, find shelter and place the casualty into a survival bag with extra clothing. Huddle together as a group and give the casualty some warm food and drink. **DO NOT**: rub the casualty, give alcohol, allow further exposure. Decide then on your next course of action. Do you go for help? or do you stay put overnight sending out the International Distress Signal? If you have to stay put overnight try and find or make adequate shelter, conserve food and drink, keep morale high, keep the casualty warm, dry and conscious, and use the International Distress Signal. If you are able to leave someone with the casualty whilst two of your party go for help from a village or farm the following information is essential; accurate location of the casualty, nature of injuries, number injured, number in group, condition of others in group (if one person is suffering it is possible that others will be too), treatment already given, and time of accident. Remember that **WET + COLD = EXPOSURE**. This rapid cooling of the inner body can lead to fatalities. **ALWAYS BE PREPARED.**

Tourist Information

(NP) = National Park. (S) = Seasonal
AMBLESIDE
The Old Courthouse, Church Street.
LA22 OBT Tel: (015394) 32582
BRAITHWAITE Whinlatter Forest
Park (Forestry Commission),
Whinlatter Pass, CA12 5TW
Tel: (017687) 78469
CARLISLE
Old Town Hall, Green Market.
CA3 8JH Tel: (01228) 512444
COCKERMOUTH
Town Hall, Market Place. CA13 9NP
Tel: (01900) 822634
EGREMONT
Lowes Court Gallery, 12 Main Street.
CA22 2DW Tel: (01946) 820693
GLENRIDDING (NP)
Beckside Car Park. CA11 0PA
Tel: (017684) 82414
GRASMERE
National Trust, The Hollens, LA22 9QZ
Tel: (015394) 35599
GRASMERE (NP) (S)
Red Bank Road. LA22 9SW
Tel: (015394) 35245
GRASMERE
National Trust Information Centre,
Church Stile. LA22 9SW
Tel: (015394) 35621
KESWICK
Moot Hall, Market Square. CA12 5JR
Tel: (017687) 72645
KESWICK (NP)
31 Lake Road. CA12 5DQ
Tel: (017687) 72803
MARYPORT
Maryport Maritime Museum,
1 Senhouse St. CA15 6AB
Tel: (01900) 813738

PENRITH
Robinson's School, Middlegate.
CA11 7PT
Tel: (01768) 867466
POOLEY BRIDGE (NP) (S)
The Square. CA10 2NW
Tel: (017684) 86530
SEATOLLER (NP) (S)
Seatoller Barn. CA12 2XN
Tel: (017687) 77294
SOUTHWAITE
M6 Service Area, South of Carlisle.
CA4 0NS
Tel: (016974) 73445/73446
WHITEHAVEN
Market Hall, Market Place. CA28 7JG
Tel: (01946) 695678

Useful Information

FELL RESCUE SERVICES
Contact the Police. Tel: 999
WEATHER FORECAST
National Park recorded information
(including details of fell-top
conditions)
Tel: (017687) 75757
RADIO CUMBRIA
Frequencies: medium 397 (North),
358 (Central & South), 206 (West),
VHF 104.2 (Central) and
95 - 96 (all other areas).
**LONG DISTANCE WALKERS
ASSOCIATION**
117 Higher Lane, Rainford, St Helens,
Merseyside, WA11 8BQ.
Tel: (01744) 882638
THE DISCOVERY VISITOR CENTRE
1 Market Place, Middleton-in-
Teesdale, Co Durham, DL12 0QG
Tel & Fax: (01833) 640638
For details of current and forthcoming
Walks of Discovery walking guides.